MERGERS AND ACQUISITIONS

IN A NUTSHELL

By

DALE A. OESTERLE
Monfort Professor of Commercial Law
Director, Entrepreneurial Law Center
University of Colorado School of Law

WEST GROUP

A THOMSON COMPANY

ST. PAUL, MINN.
2001

Nutshell Series, In a Nutshell, the Nutshell Logo and the West Group
symbol are registered trademarks used herein under license.

COPYRIGHT © 2001 By WEST GROUP
610 Opperman Drive
P.O. Box 64526
St. Paul, MN 55164–0526
1–800–328–9352

All rights reserved
Printed in the United States of America

ISBN 0–314–25315–7

TEXT IS PRINTED ON 10% POST
CONSUMER RECYCLED PAPER

1st Reprint — 2003

To my son William:

*For showing courage and pluck
at a very young age*

PREFACE

The following materials provide a summary of the legal regulation of acquisitions in the United States. Since the legal rules have largely defined acquisition structure and procedure in the United States, the materials also provide a snapshot of current acquisition practice.

The author thanks his good friend and colleague, Associate Professor Wayne M. Gazur, for authoring Chapters 7 and 8 on accounting principles and tax rules for acquisitions.

Dale Arthur Oesterle
Boulder, Colorado, 2001

ACKNOWLEDGMENTS

The author thanks Ms. Kay Wilkie for her manuscript assistance and thanks Nathan Dexter ('03) for his research assistance.

TABLE OF CASES

References are to Pages

TABLE OF CASES

TABLE OF CASES

TABLE OF CASES

TABLE OF CASES

OUTLINE

PART I.   THE BASICS OF A CORPORATE ACQUISITION

PART II. LEGAL RULES AFFECTING THE CHOICE OF ACQUISITION FORM

OUTLINE

PART III. THE LEGAL POWER AND DUTIES OF BOARDS OF DIRECTORS AND CONTROLLING SHAREHOLDERS IN ACQUISITIONS

OUTLINE

ABBREVIATIONS

ADSP	— Aggregate Deemed Sales Price
AGUB	— Adjusted Grossed-Up Basis
Amex	— American (Stock) Exchange
APB	— Accounting Principles Board
CBOE	— Chicago Board Options Exchange
CFIUS	— Committee on Foreign Investment in the U.S.
CGCL	— California General Corporation Law
DGCL	— Delaware General Corporation Law
DOJ	— Department of Justice
EBITDA	— Earnings Before Interest, Tax, Depreciation and Amortization
ECNs	— Electronic Trading Systems
FAS	— Financial Accounting Statement
FASB	— Financial Accounting Standards Board
FTC	— Federal Trade Commission
GAAP	— Generally Accepted Accounting Principles
HHI	— Herfindahl-Hirschman Index
HSR	— Hart-Scott-Rodino (Act)
IRC	— Internal Revenue Code
MBCA	— Model Business Corporation Act
NASDAQ	— National Association of Securities Dealers Automatic Quotation System
NJSA	— New Jersey Statutes Annotated
NLRA	— National Labor Relations Act
NYCLA	— New York Consolidated Laws Annotated
NYSE	— New York Stock Exchange
ORCA	— Ohio Revised Code Annotated
PCSA	— Pennsylvania Consolidated Statutes Annot.
Rel.	— (SEC) Release
RMBCA	— Revised Model Business Corporation Act
SA	— Securities Act of 1933
SEA	— Securities Exchange Act of 1934
SEC	— Securities and Exchange Commission
UFCA	— Uniform Fraud Conveyance Act
UFTA	— Uniform Fraud Transfer Act

RESEARCH REFERENCES

Key Number System: Agriculture ⇐6 (23k6); Associations ⇐23 (41k23); Banks and Banking ⇐67, 283, 307, 315.5 (52k67, 52k283, 52k307, 52k315.5); Beneficial Associations ⇐15 (54k15); Building and Loan Associations ⇐44 (66k44); Carriers ⇐17 (70k17); Clubs ⇐14 (80k14); Corporations ⇐581–591, 690 (101k581–101k591, 101k690); Counties ⇐11 (104k111); Electricity 2.1 (134kl2.1); Insurance ⇐1159, 1189, 1216, 1231, 1248, 1263, 1278, 1289, 1325 (217k1159, 217k1189, 217k1216, 217k1231, 217k1248, 217k1263, 217k1278, 217k1289, 21kk1325); Internal Revenue ⇐3660–3686 (220k3660–220k3686); Joint Stock Companies and Business Trusts ⇐22 (225k22); Municipal Corporations ⇐31 (268k31); Partnership ⇐349 (289k349); Railroads ⇐13 (320k13); Securities Regulation ⇐60.22, 60.28(15) (349Bk60.22, 349Bk60.28(15)); Taxation ⇐999 (371k999); Telecommunications ⇐45 (372k45)

Am Jur 2d, Bankruptcy §§ 1509-1517; Banks and Financial Institutions §§ 192-200; Business Trusts §§ 95-97; Carriers §§ 55-62; Corporations §§ 463-577, 2077-2080, 2608-2653, 2680-2686, 2701-2703; Energy and Power Sources § 172; Foreign Corporations §§ 394-398; Municipal Corporations, Counties, and Other Political Subdivisions § 38; Securities Regulation-Federal §§ 1141-1148; Securities Regulation-State § 147

Corpus Juris Secundum, Aeronautics and Aerospace § 183; Agriculture §§ 130, 139; Associations §§ 54-59; Bankruptcy §§ 368-415; Banks and Banking §§ 155-162; Beneficial Associations § 10; Carriers § 261; Clubs § 17; Corporations §§ 792-810, 931-935; Insurance §§ 123-126; Municipal Corporations § 96; Railroads §§ 339, 342.1; Street and Urban Railroads § 14

ALR Index: Consolidation and Merger; Reorganization

ALR Digest: Bankruptcy §§ 81-97; Banks § 188; Corporations §§ 30-40; Income Taxes §§ 49, 55; Merger §§ 1 et seq.; Street Railways § 24

Am Jur Legal Forms 2d, Bankruptcy §§ 37:171-37:173; Banks §§ 38:91-38:120; Building and Savings and Loan Associations §§ 48:12-48:22; Business Franchises § 50:39; Corporations §§ 74:2081-74:2120, 74:2651-74:2848, 74:2941-74:2979; Insurance §§ 149:31-149:38; Trusts § 251:734

Am Jur Pleading and Practice (Rev), Bankruptcy §§ 10, 11, 593 et seq.; Corporations §§ 332-371; Monopolies, Restraints of Trade, and Unfair Trade Practices §§ 49, 59; Railroads §§ 80-86; Securities Regulation § 57.5

57 Am Jur Trials 1, Private Cost Recovery Actions Under CERCLA; 24 Am Jur Trials 1, Defending

Antitrust Lawsuits; 10 Am Jur Trials 445, Handling Motor Carrier Merger Applications

34 POF3d 387, CERCLA Liability of Parent, Subsidiary and Successor Corporations

46 POF2d 313, Products Liability: Continuation of Business Enterprise or Product Line by Successor Corporation; 24 POF2d 71, Proper Purpose for Shareholder's Inspection of Corporate Books and Records; 20 POF2d 609, De Facto Merger of Two Corporations; 6 POF2d 387, Dissension or Deadlock of Corporate Directors or Shareholders; 5 POF2d 645, Oppressive Conduct by Majority Shareholders, Directors, or Those in Control of Corporation

*

MERGERS AND ACQUISITIONS

IN A NUTSHELL

*

PART I.   THE BASICS OF A CORPORATE ACQUISITION

CHAPTER 1

THE PRIMARY TYPES OF CORPORATE ACQUISITIONS

Corporations are artificial legal entities. They must be created and empowered by legislative authority. In the United States, unlike most other countries of the world, individual states charter corporations at the request of groups of individuals, *incorporators*. All states now use a registration system; that is, if the papers filed by incorporators meet minimal, objective administrative standards, a state official must give official recognition to the new corporate entity.

The state corporate codes provide the fundamental authorization for corporations to enter into major corporate acquisitions. Moreover, the state codes specify the internal procedures required for corporations participating in acquisitions. The provisions on acquisitions of our 50 state corporate codes give corporate acquisitions in the United States their basic structure and, therefore, their basic legal nomenclature. The statutory definitions depend more on the *procedure* constituent parties use to effect the transaction than the end position of the parties.

Since the beginning of this century the tiny state of Delaware has been the most popular jurisdiction of incorporation for large, publicly-traded multistate corporations. Almost 60 percent of our 500 largest corporations and almost one-half of the corporations listed on the New York Stock Exchange are Delaware corporations. Relative to most other states, Delaware's basic corporate code, entitled the "Delaware General Corporation Law," gives more leeway to corporate managers in their operation of the firm's business.

Perhaps the most important illustration of Delaware's enhanced flexibility is in its provisions on mergers and acquisitions. Indeed the differences are so pronounced in the acquisition sections that one often finds large firms changing their place of incorporation to Delaware on the eve of a major acquisition to take advantage of the Delaware provisions. Sections of the Delaware corporate code will be referenced as "DGCL §."

The structure of the DGCL is typical of the structure of most state corporate codes. The authority and procedure for effecting a *statutory merger* is outlined in § 251, and the legal effect of a merger is detailed in §§ 259 to 261. A special *short-form* merger procedure for some parent-subsidiary mergers is contained in § 253. The code covers mergers between domestic and foreign corporations (corporations incorporated in other states) in § 252 and mergers between corporations and limited liability companies (an artificial legal entity registered under a separate enabling act) in § 264.

There is also an abbreviated procedure for cash mergers in § 251(f). The procedure for an *asset sale* is contained in § 271. The appraisal rights of dissenting shareholders are outlined in § 262. Delaware regulates single-firm reorganizations of capital structure in § 242, which specifies the requirements for amending a corporation's certificate of incorporation. The only provision specific to *stock acquisitions* is § 203 that limits hostile tender offers.

Delaware also has developed a sophisticated body of precedent on corporate law issues, because of the expertise of the judges in a limited jurisdiction trial court, the Delaware Court of Chancery, and of the justices in the Delaware Supreme Court, who hear appeals from the Chancery Court. This body of case law precedent has proven to be particularly important in acquisitions that often cause disgruntled shareholders to take their grievances to court. The Delaware case law controls Delaware corporations and is often viewed as significant precedent by the courts of other states dealing with their domestically incorporated firms. As a consequence, this Nutshell will often feature and discuss Delaware court cases.

At the other end of the spectrum is California's corporate code, which features a heavier regulatory hand. Its acquisition provisions give shareholders of constituent corporations their strongest set of voting and appraisal rights, for example. As a consequence, very few of our large multistate corporations are incorporated in California. California does, however, usually have one of the highest numbers of annual incorporations of all the states because of the many new small businesses formed in the state. Most states fall somewhere between the Delaware and California models.

The Committee on Corporate Laws of the Section of Corporation, Banking and Business Law of the American Bar Association, in partnership with the American Law Institute, exerts a very significant influence on the content of many state corporate codes. The committee has developed and periodically revises a Model Business Corporation Act (hereafter cited as the MBCA). Over 35 states have used one of the versions of the MBCA as a basis for their local codes, and states scrutinize each new revision of sections in the MBCA with an eye to adopting the most modern provisions. The ABA has made a proposed major revision to the Model Act in 1998 and 1999 relevant to mergers and acquisitions.

This Nutshell will feature the provisions of the DGCL and the MBCA on mergers and acquisitions. Brief mention is also made of the California provisions.

§ 1. The Statutory Merger or Consolidation

Stock Swap Statutory Merger. Diagram 1
shows a stock swap statutory merger. Two corporations, A Corp and B Corp, start as separate legal
entities with separate owners, their shareholders.
In the transaction, B Corp merges into A Corp and
A Corp is the survivor.

There are other structural options. A Corp
could also merge into B Corp, or A Corp and B
Corp could merge into a new corporation formed
for the transaction, C Corp, in a *consolidation.*

In the merger in Diagram 1, B Corp shareholders' stock is cancelled and they receive as
consideration A Corp shares. It is, therefore, a
stock-for-stock merger (or a stock swap merger). A
Corp absorbs the assets and liabilities of B Corp
"as a matter of law." We will investigate further
what this means in the chapter on successor
liability.

After the merger closes, only A Corp survives;
B Corp is extinguished. The shareholders of A Corp
continue to hold their stock as before and the
shareholders of old B Corp now hold newly-issued
additional A Corp stock; the ownership interests of
A Corp and B Corp are pooled in the survivor. A
Corp now has added the assets and liabilities of old
B Corp to A Corp's original assets and liabilities;
the assets and liabilities of both constituent
corporations are pooled.

Diagram 1.
The Plain-Vanilla Statutory Merger:
Stock for Stock*

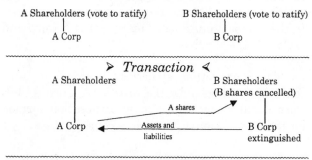

> ➤ *Pre-Transaction* ◄

A Shareholders (vote to ratify)   B Shareholders (vote to ratify)

A Corp   B Corp

> ➤ *Transaction* ◄

A Shareholders   B Shareholders
                          (B shares cancelled)

A shares

A Corp   Assets and   B Corp
              liabilities   extinguished

> ➤ *Post-Transaction* ◄

A Shareholders (original A shareholders plus old B shareholders)

A Corp   (A assets and liabilities combined with old B Corp
             assets and liabilities)

---

* This is a tax-free merger (an A reorganization).

Cash-out Statutory Mergers. In a *cash-out transaction,* the purchasing firm does not want the shareholders of the selling firm to end up holding voting common stock in the purchasing firm. The purchasing firm wants to pay cash for the selling firm or, if cash is not available, to pay the selling firm shareholders in non-voting investments in the purchasing firm—debentures (debt) or non-voting preferred or common stock (equity). For a cash-out statutory merger, start with Diagram 1 and replace the A Corp shares going to the B Corp shareholders with cash. See Diagram 2.

Diagram 2.
Cash-Out Merger*

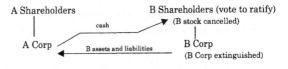

* This is a taxable transaction.

Required Procedure for a Statutory Merger. If both A Corp and B Corp are Delaware corporations, DGCL § 251 controls the acquisition. Section 251(a) authorizes both firms to engage in the transaction and § 251(b) requires that the board of directors of both firms pass a resolution approving an *Agreement of Merger.* The agreement states the terms and conditions of the merger and whether the certification of incorporation of the survivor is amended. Both constituent corporations, A Corp and B Corp, then must submit the agreement to a shareholder vote under § 251(c). A majority of all the *outstanding* shares entitled to vote must ratify the agreement. (MBCA § 11.04(e) reduces the voting requirement to a majority of those present at the shareholders' meeting if a quorum exists.) The shareholders of neither constituent corporation can initiate the acquisition vote nor can they amend the agreement; it is an up or down ratifying vote. After the vote, the agreement (or a summary of the agreement entitled a "Certificate of Merger") is filed with the Delaware Secretary of State to become effective on a date specified in the near future. On that date representatives of the constituent corporations meet and close the transaction.

The mechanics of who votes in statutory mergers deserves special mention. See also Part II, Chapter 4, § 12. In Delaware the default rule is that shares that do not have general voting rights (non-voting common shares and preferred shares with no voting rights unless there are dividend arrearages) do not vote in major transactions. This seems harsh and the majority of other states do not follow Delaware's example. See MBCA § 11.04(f) (class voting mandatory on statutory mergers). Yet it is important to note that the preferred stock contracts in Delaware firms can and often do provide preferred stock shareholders a class vote in acquisitions. The Delaware voting rights of preferred stockholders can be augmented in the preferred stock investment contract. Moreover, the minimum vote required in the Delaware statutes is a majority of the outstanding shares, whether or not the shares are represented at the shareholder meeting. Since the turnout at shareholder meetings is often less than 75 percent of the outstanding voting shares, a successful vote on a merger can require an affirmative vote of well over a majority of those represented at or attending the shareholders' meeting (67 percent of the shares present if only 75 percent of the outstanding shares are represented, for example).

There are three major exceptions to the voting procedures noted above. First, in DGCL § 251(f), the shareholders of the surviving firm in a statutory merger—A Corp in Diagram 1—do not have a right to vote if the rights, preferences and privileges of their shares survive the merger (their investment contract has not changed) and if their shares are not diluted by more than a specified amount. The acquiring company cannot issue to new shareholders an amount of shares that exceeds 20 percent of the number of voting shares of A Corp outstanding before the transaction. That is, the original A Corp shareholders must hold at least 83 percent of the A Corp voting shares (5/6ths) at the conclusion of the transaction. The legislatures design the exception to recognize that when larger firms merge with much smaller firms the transaction is more a purchase of the smaller firm than a merger and the larger firm's shareholders need not ratify the transaction. Some refer to the exception as the *small-scale merger exception.*

The second exception to the voting rules is for the statutory merger of a parent corporation and a subsidiary when the parent holds over 90 percent of the subsidiary's stock. Section 253 of the DGCL permits the merger of the subsidiary into the parent (an *upstream merger*) solely on a resolution of the parent's board of directors. The shareholders of neither subsidiary nor parent have a right to vote on the transaction. (MBCA § 11.04(g) gives shareholders of the parent the right to vote if the parent issues stock in the parent to sub shareholders that carries more than 20 percent of the voting power in the parent.) Many refer to the exception as the *parent-sub merger exception.* If the subsidiary is the surviving corporation (a *downstream merger*), the shareholders of the parent corporation are entitled to vote. The ABA has a similar requirement (MBCA § 11.04 (1999 rev.)).

The third exception is still novel to Delaware, although it is likely that other states will eventually follow suit. In § 251(g) of the DGCL, no shareholder voting is required in specified reorganizations of holding companies or in specified creations of holding company structure—the *holding company exception.*

§ 2.   The Asset Acquisition

Cash-for-Assets Acquisition. Diagram 3 shows a cash-for-assets acquisition. In the first step of the transaction, A Corp pays B Corp cash consideration for B Corp's assets. A Corp may choose to accept B Corp's liabilities, offsetting the liabilities against the cash price, but A Corp does not have to do so. There is no change in the constitutional documents of A or B Corp, nor is there any change in the shares outstanding in either corporation. In the optional, but commonplace, second step of the transaction, B Corp dissolves. The B Corp charter is cancelled and B Corp shares are extinguished. After paying any residual liabilities not assumed by A Corp, the assets held by B Corp and the cash received in the transaction from A Corp are transferred to the B Corp shareholders in a liquidating distribution. The investment contract held by A Corp shareholders (the rights and privileges attached to the A Corp shares) and A Corp's constitutional document (its certificate of incorporation) are unchanged.

Diagram 3.
The Common Asset Acquisition:
Cash for Assets with the Selling
Corporation Dissolving*

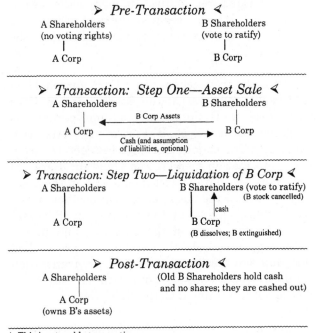

➢ *Pre-Transaction* ◄

A Shareholders
(no voting rights)

A Corp

B Shareholders
(vote to ratify)

B Corp

➢ *Transaction: Step One—Asset Sale* ◄

A Shareholders

A Corp

B Corp Assets

Cash (and assumption
of liabilities, optional)

B Shareholders

B Corp

➢ *Transaction: Step Two—Liquidation of B Corp* ◄

A Shareholders

A Corp

B Shareholders (vote to ratify)
(B stock cancelled)

cash

B Corp
(B dissolves; B extinguished)

➢ *Post-Transaction* ◄

A Shareholders

A Corp
(owns B's assets)

(Old B Shareholders hold cash
and no shares; they are cashed out)

* This is a taxable transaction.

After an asset acquisition, B Corp must either reinvest the cash received in operating assets or dissolve and pass the cash in a liquidation distribution back to its shareholders. If B Corp invests the cash in assets generating passive income— income from the management efforts of others, such as stocks, bonds or rental property—the Internal Revenue Code deems B Corp a personal holding company, which has tax consequences that can be onerous, and the acquisition also cannot qualify for tax-free status. In most asset acquisitions then, B Corp dissolves after the acquisition. The B Corp shareholders vote a second time on the dissolution.

After the transaction, old B Corp shareholders hold cash consideration (no shares) and A Corp holds title to B Corp's assets (and perhaps is obligated on some of B Corp's pre-transaction liabilities). The major differences between Diagram 1, the stock swap merger, and Diagram 3 are: (a) who votes—A shareholders do not vote in the asset acquisition; (b) the post-transaction position of the old B shareholders—in the merger the B shareholders hold shares in the survivor, and in the asset acquisition the B shareholders are cashed out; and (c) the location of B's pre-transaction liabilities—in an asset acquisition A Corp may choose not to assume B Corp's liabilities.

For a *stock-for-assets acquisition*, start with Diagram 3. Replace the cash consideration going to B Corp with A Corp common stock. Moreover, assume A Corp not only buys all of B Corp's assets but also assumes all of B Corp's liabilities. See Diagram 4 below. The end result is identical to the post-transaction position in Diagram 1. The shareholders of the constituent firms have pooled their ownership interests in a corporation that itself has the combined assets and liabilities of both firms.

Diagram 4.
Stock-for-Assets Acquisition*

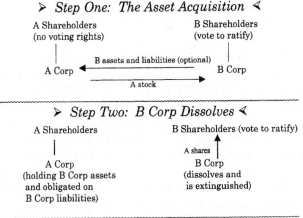

➢ *Step One: The Asset Acquisition* ◄

A Shareholders
(no voting rights)

B Shareholders
(vote to ratify)

B assets and liabilities (optional)

A Corp ◄——————————————————————► B Corp

A stock

➢ *Step Two: B Corp Dissolves* ◄

A Shareholders

B Shareholders (vote to ratify)

A shares

A Corp
(holding B Corp assets
and obligated on
B Corp liabilities)

B Corp
(dissolves and
is extinguished)

---

* This is a tax-free stock acquisition (a C reorganization).

Procedure for a Stock Acquisition. If both A Corp and B Corp are Delaware corporations, the transaction is controlled by DGCL §§ 122 and 271. Section 122(4) is a general grant of power to Delaware corporations; the provision empowers A Corp to buy assets and B Corp to sell assets. Another general grant of power, § 122(13), authorizes A Corp to assume B Corp's liabilities. Section 271, however, is specific to asset acquisitions and conditions B Corp's general authority to sell its assets on a ratifying shareholder vote. Under § 271, B Corp's board of directors, whenever it resolves to have the corporation sell "all or substantially all" of B Corp's assets, must submit a resolution to its shareholders and a majority of the outstanding shares entitled to vote must ratify the transaction. B Corp's shareholders cannot initiate the transaction nor can they amend the acquisition agreement. A Corp shareholders are not entitled to vote on the transaction.

The question of what constitutes "substantially all" of the corporate assets under § 271 is colored by whether "the sale of assets [is] quantitatively vital to the operation of the corporation and is out of the ordinary and substantially affects the existence and purpose of the corporation." *Gimbel v. Signal Companies, Inc.* (Del. Ch. 1974). See also *Thorpe v. CERBCO, Inc.* (Del. 1996) (sale of stock in subsidiary was 68 percent of parents' assets and primary income-generating asset did require a shareholder vote). MBCA § 12.02(a) replaces the "all or substantially all" standard with one that catches any "disposition [that] would leave the corporation without a significant continuing business activity." The section has a safe harbor. A significant business activity remains if the continuing business activity represents at least 25 percent of the total assets and 25 percent of either income (before income taxes) or revenues from pre-transaction operations.

If B Corp dissolves, a board resolution on dissolution is submitted to B Corp shareholders under DGCL § 275 and a majority of the out-standing shares entitled to vote must ratify the resolution. A certificate of dissolution is then sent to the Delaware Secretary of State. On the effective date of the dissolution, the corporation is dissolved and its stock extinguished. The corporation then has three years to wind up, paying its liabilities and passing back to shareholders any residual cash surplus.

§ 3. The Stock Acquisition

Cash-for-Stock Acquisition. In a cash-for-stock acquisition, A Corp buys B Corp stock directly from B Corp shareholders in exchange for cash. See Diagram 5 below.

After the transaction, A Corp owns the B Corp stock; A Corp is the *parent* corporation of a new *subsidiary* corporation, B Corp. Old B Corp share-holders have tendered and exchanged their shares for cash. There is no change in the certificates of incorporation of either A Corp or B Corp, nor is there any change in the investment contracts represented by an A Corp share and a B Corp share. Only the owner of the B Corp shares has changed. If A Corp cannot convince all the B shareholders to tender their shares for the cash consideration, then a minority block of B Corp stock remains out-standing. B Corp would not be a *wholly-owned subsidiary* but a *partially-owned subsidiary*.

Diagram 5.
The Basic Stock Acquisition: Cash for Stock*

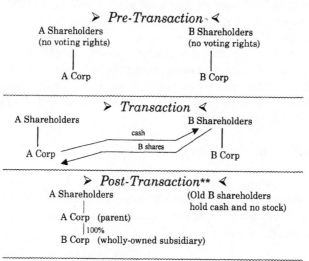

➢ *Pre-Transaction* ◄

A Shareholders
(no voting rights)

B Shareholders
(no voting rights)

A Corp

B Corp

➢ *Transaction* ◄

A Shareholders

B Shareholders

cash

B shares

A Corp

B Corp

➢ *Post-Transaction*** ◄

A Shareholders

(Old B shareholders
hold cash and no stock)

A Corp   (parent)

│ 100%

B Corp   (wholly-owned subsidiary)

---

* This is a taxable transaction.
** This assumes *all* the B shareholders voluntarily took the cash in exchange for their shares.

For a *stock-for-stock acquisition*, start with Diagram 5. Replace the cash consideration going to B Corp shareholders with A Corp common stock. See Diagram 6. The end result is similar to the post-transaction position in Diagram 1 except that A Corp holds B Corp's assets and liabilities in a wholly-owned subsidiary, a separate legal entity, rather than having combined the B Corp assets and liabilities with A Corp assets and liabilities in one legal entity. The advantage of the parent-subsidiary structure is that the B Corp creditors of the subsidiary do not have a claim on A Corp assets held by the parent. If, however, one wants a structure identical to the post-transaction structure in Diagram 1, one need only merge the wholly-owned subsidiary into the parent with a simple board of directors' resolution.

Diagram 6.
Stock-for-Stock Acquisition*

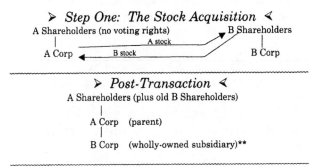

➤ *Step One: The Stock Acquisition* ◀

A Shareholders (no voting rights)   B Shareholders

| A stock

A Corp ◄——— B stock ———   B Corp

➤ *Post-Transaction* ◀

A Shareholders (plus old B Shareholders)

|

A Corp   (parent)

|

B Corp   (wholly-owned subsidiary)**

* This is a tax-free stock acquisition (a B reorganization).
** This assumes that all B shareholders tender their shares.

Procedure for a Stock Acquisition. If both A Corp and B Corp are Delaware corporations, the authority for A Corp to purchase and hold the stock of another corporation is found in DGCL §§ 122(4) and (11) on general corporate powers. DGCL § 122(10) also empowers A Corp to manage the affairs of B Corp. Neither the shareholders of A Corp nor of B Corp have, under any provision of the DGCL, a right to vote on the stock acquisition. In theory, B Corp shareholders do not need the protection of a right to vote because they individually decide whether or not to accept the consideration offered by A Corp for their shares. Their right to refuse the offer is a substitute for their right to dissent in a vote.

In all but a few states, the shareholders in the purchasing corporation do not have the right to vote on the transaction nor to claim appraisal rights. The states that give shareholders in the purchasing firm voting rights in stock-for-stock acquisitions, based on the voting power of the stock issued for use as consideration, are California, New Jersey, Ohio and Rhode Island. See also MBCA § 6.21. The New York Stock Exchange listing requirements also require that shareholders of the acquiring corporation vote on the acquisition if more than 20 percent of a corporation's outstanding shares are offered to target shareholders in a stock-for-stock acquisition.

There is a specialized section in the DGCL, however, § 203, that applies to stock acquisitions for publicly-traded companies. Within the last 10 years, most states (at last count the number was over 40) have passed *anti-takeover statutes* that restrain stock acquisitions of publicly-traded companies. Delaware's § 203 is such a statute. Most anti-takeover statutes give target shareholders voting rights, not on the stock acquisition itself but on the effect of the acquisition. If the target board

disapproves of the stock acquisition, the shareholders may, for example, vote on whether the
stock acquired by the bidder can vote or on
whether the bidder can, subsequent to a stock
acquisition in which some shareholders do not sell
into the offer, execute a second-stage, cash-out
statutory merger to gain 100 percent of the target
stock. Delaware's section, known as a *business
combination* or *freeze-out* statute, is of the latter
ilk. Of course, by severely restricting the effect of
an acquisition, the legislation in essence regulates
the acquisition itself. Indeed it would perhaps be
more honest and understandable simply to
condition stock acquisitions on a shareholder vote.

§ 4.   The Statutory Share Exchange

The MBCA follows the basic organization in
the DGCL with a minor addition. Section 11.03
provides a procedure for a statutory *share exchange* (often called a *compulsory share exchange*).
In a statutory share exchange, one firm acquires
all of the outstanding stock in a second firm
through an affirmative shareholder vote of the
seller. It contrasts with a typical stock acquisition
in which the purchasing firm makes offers to buy
shares that each shareholder may accept or reject.
A majority of the shareholders of the acquired firm
must approve a statutory share exchange; a
majority of the shareholders of the acquiring firm
need approve the exchange only if acquired-firm
shareholders receive a substantial number of
shares in the acquiring firm (usually an amount

equal to 20 percent or more of the number of shares outstanding before the acquisition). A dissenting shareholder in the acquiring corporation may vote no, but if she loses the vote she must turn over her shares to the acquiring corporation; the exchange is *compulsory* on an affirmative majority shareholder vote. Over 20 states have adopted such a provision, yet few practitioners use the procedure. The light use of the procedure is due to its poor comparison with a *triangular statutory merger*, an acquisition structure we investigate below.

§ 5. Special Applications of the Basic Transactional Forms: Two-Stage Stock Acquisitions, Single-Firm Recapitalizations, Triangular Acquisitions and Leveraged Buy-Outs

Two-Stage Stock Acquisitions. Many stock acquisitions are *two-stage acquisitions*, in which the stock acquisition is followed by a *back-end merger*. In the second stage the purchasing corporation *drops down* a subsidiary and merges the subsidiary with the partially-owned target. See Diagram 7.

The second stage of the transaction is known as a *squeeze-out* (or, less frequently, as a *freeze-out*). In a typical squeeze-out, a corporation holding shares in a partially-owned subsidiary drops down a new wholly-owned shell subsidiary and merges the partially-owned sub into the wholly-owned sub

Diagram 7.
Two-Stage Acquisition: Stock Acquisition Followed by a Squeeze-Out Statutory Merger

➤ *Stage One: Stock Acquisition* ◄

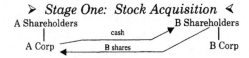

A Shareholders
|
A Corp

cash
B shares

B Shareholders

B Corp

➤ *Post-Stage One: A Partially-Owned Subsidiary* ◄

A Shareholders
|
A Corp (owns 51% or more of outstanding B shares)
|
B Corp (minority B shareholders own
49% or less of outstanding B shares)

➤ *Stage Two: A Squeeze-Out Merger* ◄

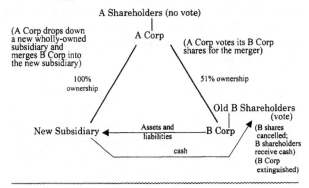

A Shareholders (no vote)
|
A Corp

(A Corp drops down a new wholly-owned subsidiary and merges B Corp into the new subsidiary)

(A Corp votes its B Corp shares for the merger)

100% ownership

51% ownership

New Subsidiary

Assets and liabilities

cash

B Corp

Old B Shareholders (vote)

(B shares cancelled; B shareholders receive cash)
(B Corp extinguished)

➤ *Post-Stage Two* ◄

A Shareholders
|
(parent)   A Corp
|
(wholly-owned subsidiary)   B Corp   (new subsidiary changes name to B Corp)

(see Diagram 7, Stage Two). In a *drop-down* the purchasing corporation itself acts as an incorporator for a new corporation, usually a *shell* corporation, one that has no assets. The constituent parties to the back-end merger are the wholly-owned shell subsidiary of the purchasing corporation and the newly acquired, partially-owned subsidiary that was the target of the stock acquisition. The firm gives the minority shareholders in the partially-owned subsidiary cash or debt securities (debentures) in A Corp for the cancelled shares.

The purpose of such an acquisition is often speed—the purchasing firm can gain control of the target faster because it can close the first stage faster than a statutory merger or asset sale. The second stage, the *squeeze-out*, is necessary to convert a partially-owned subsidiary to a wholly-owned subsidiary.

In Delaware corporations, shareholders of the parent corporation have no voting or appraisal rights in either the stock acquisition or the second stage, back-end merger. California and other states, however, give shareholders in the purchasing firm voting rights in the first or second stage if the purchasing firm will issue stock in either transaction that dilutes the voting power of its pre-existing shareholders by more than five-sixths. CGCL §§ 1200(b), (e) and 1201. See also RMBCA § 6.21.

Single-Firm Recapitalizations. In another, more notorious type of squeeze-out, a corporation

Diagram 8.
Recapitalizations: A Statutory Merger as an Alternative to a Charter Amendment

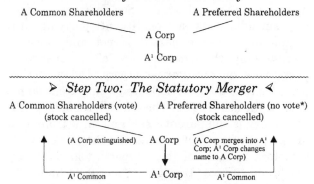

> ➤ *Step One: A Corp Drops Down* ◄
> *a Wholly-Owned Subsidiary*

A Common Shareholders   A Preferred Shareholders

A Corp

A¹ Corp

> ➤ *Step Two: The Statutory Merger* ◄

A Common Shareholders (vote)   A Preferred Shareholders (no vote*)
(stock cancelled)   (stock cancelled)

(A Corp extinguished)   A Corp   (A Corp merges into A¹ Corp; A¹ Corp changes name to A Corp)

A¹ Common   A¹ Corp   A¹ Common

> ➤ *Post-Transaction* ◄

A Shareholders (all common shares)

A Corp

---

*   In Delaware, the preferred shareholders do not vote on the merger unless their voting rights are expressly provided for in the certificate of incorporation. Under the MBCA, the preferred shareholders vote as a class.

with a minority block of shareholders undertakes a single-firm recapitalization through a statutory merger. The firm drops down a new wholly-owned shell subsidiary and merges itself into the subsidiary. See Diagram 8. All of the stock in the corporation is cancelled. The majority shareholders in the original firm receive stock in the surviving firm and the minority shareholders receive cash or debt securities.

Triangular Acquisitions. In triangular statutory mergers, the purchasing firm drops down a wholly-owned subsidiary and the selling firm merges with the subsidiary. See Diagram 9. Since the subsidiary is a constituent party to the acquisition and the parent is not and since by statute only the shareholders of a constituent party vote on statutory mergers, Delaware law provides that the shareholders of the parent do not vote on the acquisition. The only shareholder of the subsidiary is the parent itself and, in a triangular merger, the board of directors of the parent votes the stock in favor of the merger by simple board resolution. Since triangular mergers limit the voting rights of purchasing shareholders and isolate the newly-absorbed selling company liabilities in a subsidiary, free from the purchasing company assets, triangular mergers have become a very popular method of acquisition. Again, the California general corporate code is not in accord, giving shareholders in the parent voting rights if parent stock is issued to target firm shareholders and dilutes the pre-existing shareholders' voting power by over five-sixths. CGCL §§ 1200(e) and 1201. See also MBCA § 6.21.

Triangular statutory mergers are known as *forward triangular mergers* when the target merges into the shell subsidiary and *reverse*

Diagram 9.
Forward Triangular Merger*

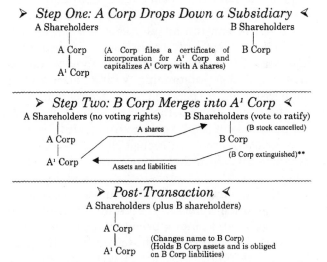

➤ *Step One: A Corp Drops Down a Subsidiary* ◄

A Shareholders   B Shareholders

A Corp   (A Corp files a certificate of   B Corp
              incorporation for A¹ Corp and
              capitalizes A¹ Corp with A shares)
A¹ Corp

➤ *Step Two: B Corp Merges into A¹ Corp* ◄

A Shareholders (no voting rights)   B Shareholders (vote to ratify)

                    A shares   (B stock cancelled)
A Corp   B Corp
                                                (B Corp extinguished)**
A¹ Corp   Assets and liabilities

➤ *Post-Transaction* ◄

A Shareholders (plus B shareholders)

A Corp
              (Changes name to B Corp)
A¹ Corp   (Holds B Corp assets and is obliged
              on B Corp liabilities)

---

* This is a tax-free merger (an A(2)(D) reorganization). If B share-holders receive cash for their shares instead of A Corp shares, it is a taxable exchange.

** It would be a reverse triangular merger if A¹ Corp merged into B Corp with B Corp surviving. In the exchange, B shareholders all receive A shares (or cash) and A Corp, the shareholders of A¹ Corp, receives the only remaining B Corp shares.

triangular mergers when the shell subsidiary merges into the target. A less popular triangular acquisition is the *triangular asset acquisition*. In a triangular asset acquisition, the purchaser drops down a shell subsidiary that purchases the assets of the target and the target dissolves.

Leveraged Buy-Out (LBO). In a leveraged buy-out a group of investors, led by a leveraged buy-out fund (a private limited partnership), creates an acquisition vehicle (a shell corporation) and funds the entity with some cash. The acquisition vehicle then raises a substantial additional amount of cash by selling debt to banks and institutional investors. The vehicle uses its cash to purchase 50 percent of the outstanding voting shares of a publicly-traded corporation. The acquisition vehicle then merges into the target. The remaining voting shares of the target are exchanged for debt or non-voting preferred securities (the vehicle has exhausted its cash) and the owners of the acquisition vehicle take the only stock outstanding in the target. The surviving target assumes the debt of the acquisition vehicle. The result transforms a public corporation into a privately-held one with a significantly increased debt-to-equity ratio. See *Pay 'N Pak Stores v. Court Square Capital LTD* (9th Cir. 1998). The new owners massage the assets of the target, selling some and increasing the cash flow of others, to service the new debt. If the new owners overpaid for the target and cannot service the new debt, the target must go through a bankruptcy reorganization, known as a *Chapter 11 proceeding.*

To pay back the new loans, the target will (1) sell new bonds, (2) reduce expenses, and (3) sell some assets.

Diagram 10.
Leveraged Buy-Out (LBO)

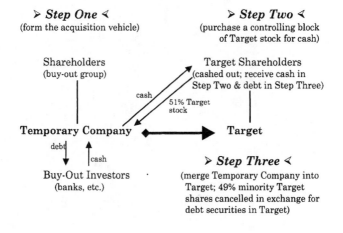

> *Step One* ◄
(form the acquisition vehicle)

> *Step Two* ◄
(purchase a controlling block of Target stock for cash)

Shareholders
(buy-out group)

Target Shareholders
(cashed out; receive cash in Step Two & debt in Step Three)

cash

51% Target stock

Temporary Company

Target

debt

cash

Buy-Out Investors
(banks, etc.)

> *Step Three* ◄
(merge Temporary Company into Target; 49% minority Target shares cancelled in exchange for debt securities in Target)

CHAPTER 2

THE ACQUISITION PROCESS AND ITS BASIC LEGAL DOCUMENTS

§ 6. The Chronology of a Typical Negotiated Acquisition for a Privately-Held Company

A privately-held company is one that does not have public, periodic reporting requirements under the Securities and Exchange Act of 1934 (hereafter SEA). SEA § 12. That is, the company is not traded on any national stock exchanges and has fewer than 500 shareholders or less than $10 million in assets. Most privately-held companies are much smaller than publicly-held companies. Privately-held companies commonly take the following path in their acquisition negotiations.

In a negotiated purchase of a privately-held company, the CEOs (Chief Executive Officers) of the two constituent corporations first meet and mutually agree on the potential success of further negotiation and on ballpark financial terms for a deal. These preliminary negotiations are often embodied in a non-binding *Letter of Intent*. Most CEOs receive advice from their internal financial experts, usually the firm's CFO (Chief Financial Officer), and, although less often, from outside investment bankers and accountants with whom they have had a prior long-standing relationship.

The preliminary agreement leads to the formal retention, by both constituent corporations, of a bevy of experts. The corporations hire lawyers to negotiate and draft the details of the acquisition documents and investment bankers and accountants to provide valuation estimates and other financial advice. The lead acquisition planner may come from any of the three professions—law, accounting or investment banking. The buyer's lawyers and accountants perform a *due diligence* investigation of the seller. If the buyer is using its stock as the consideration in the purchase, as in a stock swap for example, the seller may also perform a limited due diligence investigation of the buyer.

In a due diligence investigation, lawyers and accountants pour over the official, internal books and records of the other party to the deal, verifying the price, checking the accuracy of factual representations, and looking for trouble spots. They are aided, in appropriate cases, by other experts, such as environmental engineers or real estate appraisers, who give assurance on matters of specific importance to the transaction.

Once the CEOs agree on a final price and on a final memorandum of the acquisition agreement, they present the agreement to their respective boards of directors. If the deal is structured as a statutory merger under state corporate codes, the agreement is entitled an *Agreement of Merger*. If the deal is structured as a stock purchase, the agreement is entitled a *Stock Purchase Agreement*. If the deal is structured as an asset acquisition, the agreement is entitled an *Asset Purchase Agreement*.

The time between the negotiation of the preliminary agreement and date of board approval varies considerably and may be from two weeks to three months. The boards of directors ask questions, make comments and, if all goes well, vote their approval of the acquisition document. Experts continue their due diligence investigations after board approvals and up until the time of the closing, verifying that the closing conditions in the agreement are satisfied.

If shareholders of one or both the constituent corporations must vote to ratify the agreement, lawyers prepare shareholder meeting notices and disclosure documents. The company formally calls a special shareholder meeting or notifies shareholders that the acquisition will be on the agenda at the firm's annual meeting. The time between the board vote and the shareholder meetings is at least 30 days and often up to three months, determined by the notice requirement in state corporate codes. If the parties need the approval of a government agency (the Federal Communications Commission for media mergers or the Comptroller of the Currency for bank mergers), the

time period is further attenuated. If things go
according to plan, the shareholders of one or both
of the constituent corporations approve the acquisition by the requisite majority, usually a majority of
the outstanding voting shares.

Twenty to thirty days after the shareholder
vote, lawyers and CEOs meet to close the transaction. At the closing, once the parties are assured
that the conditions in the acquisition agreement
are satisfied, the parties exchange the deal
consideration—cash for stock, cash for assets, or
stock for stock and so on. In statutory mergers, the
parties file the Agreement of Merger (or a short
form Certificate of Merger) with an appropriate
state official (usually the Secretary of State) that,
among other things, eliminates at least one of the
constituent corporations and names the surviving
corporation. In an asset acquisition, the selling
corporation typically files Articles of Dissolution
with the Secretary of State, dissolving the selling
corporation.

§ 7.   Pricing Issues in Stock-for-Stock
   Acquisitions

Most all negotiated acquisitions have substantial time delays between the acquisition
agreement and the closing. Some acquisition
techniques, such as cash tender offers, minimize
the time delay; others, such as stock swap mergers,
may have delays of over six months. Whenever
there is such a delay, the pricing issues are more

complex, as one party or the other will absorb the consequences of the value of the selling firm changing during the delay.

In stock swaps there is the added effect on the price of value changes in the stock of the purchasing firm. In stock swaps, the purchasing corporation exchanges its shares for shares of the selling corporation. To establish a price the two parties must come to an agreement on the relative value of the two companies. After the parties negotiate an agreement on price and establish an exchange ratio for the stock of the constituent corporations, the value of one or both of the companies may change dramatically between the time of agreement and the time of the closing. Market-wide trends, such as a substantial decline in the financial markets, industry-specific market trends and company-specific performance may all affect the value of either of the constituent corporations' stock. If the changes occur before any ratifying shareholder votes, the shareholders may reject the agreement. One can easily point to spectacular failures of large combinations to illustrate the problem (the collapse of the 1998 Tellabs/Ciena and United HealthCare/Humana mergers, for example).

Moreover, if the purchasing firm is publicly traded, the market may judge the exchange ratio harshly. More and more frequently purchasing firms in a stock swap merger are witnessing a fall in their stock price within minutes of the announcement of the transaction. The fall in stock price is due to the market's judgment that the purchaser has overpaid, diluting the value of its own stock, or that the purchaser will not be able to manage the new assets well. If the price fall in the purchasing stock is substantial, the shareholders of the selling firm taking stock in the purchasing firm in the transaction may balk. The selling firm may pressure the buyer to offer additional consideration on the threat of abandoning the transaction, exacerbating the diluting effect of the deal on the purchasing firm's shareholders.

If the firms use a *fixed exchange ratio,* that is, a stock exchange ratio that is set when the board votes on the agreement of merger and does not change through the closing, the seller's stockholders bear both general market risk and the specific risk associated with the value of the purchasing firm's stock price. A decline in the relative market value of the purchasing firm decreases the value the seller's shareholders receive at the closing. Seller shareholders may refuse to ratify the proposal if the price change precedes their shareholder meeting. The buyer, on the other hand, enjoys the certainty of the fixed exchange ratio, primarily on the effect of the deal on future earnings per share (either accretive or dilutive). The downside risk for the purchaser is that a flagging exchange value may encourage third parties to make higher, competing offers to the seller.

Thus most sellers ask for downside price protection. Buyers' traditional rebuttal is that a fixed exchange ratio reflects the inherent relationship between the constituent companies' fundamental values at the time the price is set and that this relationship should not be affected by market volatility not attributable solely to a deterioration in the quality of the buying firm's securities. If the price decline is due to industry-wide or market-wide phenomena, the seller will have experienced a comparable price decline in its stock as well and the parties should consider the economic relationship between the parties to be unchanged. Most sellers argue in response that the firms may have differing sensitivities to even market-wide price shocks.

A seller with negotiating leverage may argue, therefore, for either a *walk-away* or a *floating exchange ratio* with *a price collar*. Both devices depend on an easily ascertainable stock price for the purchaser, which usually means that the purchaser must be a publicly-traded company.

A walk-away is an express condition in the acquisition agreement that gives the seller the option to walk away from the acquisition if the market value of the purchasing firm's stock falls below a specified price level. For example, a fixed exchange ratio walk-away would permit the seller to terminate the agreement if, at the time of closing, the purchasing firm's stock has decreased by 10 percent, a *single trigger*. Some walk-away clauses have a *double trigger*—the seller may terminate the agreement if either the stock value decreases by a specified percentage or more or if the purchasing firm's stock price decreases by a specified percentage or more relative to a defined peer group of stocks in pre-selected companies.

A floating exchange ratio is a promise to fix the value offered to selling shareholders at closing (e.g., $100 per seller share). It is therefore a promise by the purchaser to tender the shares necessary at closing to equal the fixed value (e.g., $100 divided by the current market price of one purchaser share). Most floating ratios base the stock exchange ratio due on an average market price for the purchasing firm's security during a period, usually 10 to 30 trading days, prior to the closing or prior to the date on which the seller's shareholders will vote to approve the transaction. The purchasing firm bears the market risk of a decline in the price of its stock. It will have to issue more shares to each seller shareholder on any price decline.

There are two problems with a floating exchange ratio. First, the rate must be carefully calculated so it will not terminate a desirable acquisition solely due to *temporary* market fluctuations (the Brazilian *real* may be devalued and jolt the market for a short time, for example). The second problem is that a floating exchange ratio exposes the purchasing firm shareholders to the possibility of massive dilution in the value and voting power of their shares, the potential dilution being limited only by the amount by which the stock price is likely to decline.

To protect against extreme dilution, acquisition agreements with floating exchange ratios often place a cap on the maximum shares the purchaser will issue in the exchange. Selling firms will, in exchange, insist on a cap on the minimum number of shares to be delivered. The upper and lower limits, known as a *price collar*, provide upper and lower market price limits to the transaction. Selling firms may want to supplement a collar with a walk-away, if a price decline in the purchasing firm's stock causes the exchange ratio to hit the high end of the collar. Purchasing firms, in response, may want to reserve contractually the right to waive the upper collar, issuing additional shares to make the seller's shareholders whole, so as to void the seller's walk-away right and preserve the deal (a *fill-or-kill option*).

In the absence of a price collar on a floating exchange ratio, the purchaser will often demand a walk-away right based on a maximum number of shares that it is willing to issue in the transaction. Selling firms agreeing to such a walk-away may negotiate for the right to waive the requirement for additional shares under the floating exchange ratio and hold the purchasing firm to closing the transaction on the original price, a reverse fill-or-kill option.

A common alternative to the floating exchange ratio coupled with a price collar is a fixed exchange ratio that is adjusted only if the value of the purchasing firm's stock falls by (or increases by) more than a fixed percentage (e.g., plus or minus 10 percent). The adjustment can be automatic or discretionary with the purchaser, a fill-or-kill option. If automatic, the adjustment is usually capped with upper and lower limits on the number of shares the purchasing firm will have to deliver.

§ 8. Basic Acquisition Documents

Most acquisitions of privately-traded companies follow a predictable trail in the execution of the legal documents. The documents also have a predictable structure. There may be substantial variety in the detail of the documents, however.

In the preliminary negotiations one often sees a Letter of Intent, a Confidentiality Agreement and, if one of the parties is publicly traded, a public announcement. Lawyers undertaking a legal audit, also known as a legal due diligence investigation, will use an Acquisition Review Check List to prepare both for signing the acquisition agreement and the closing. The essential terms of the deal are contained in an acquisition contract that looks to an exchange of consideration on the pre-arranged closing date.

A. The Confidentiality Agreement

The Confidentiality Agreement, if used, may be the first document the parties sign in an acquisition negotiation. A good one defines categories of confidential information very broadly and obligates the buyer to keep information received from the seller in strict confidence. The agreement often limits who in the employ of the purchaser may have access to the information, specifies the location of documents containing the proprietary information, and includes relevant notice requirements. A seller should not give a prospective purchaser sensitive business information until the purchaser has signed a Confidentiality Agreement.

Sometimes the agreement is consolidated into the Letter of Intent, but many lawyers believe this is a mistake. The seller intends the Confidentiality Agreement to be an enforceable contract whether or not the parties ever execute a Letter of Intent and, if executed, whether or not the Letter of Intent is legally binding. When the parties sign a definitive acquisition agreement, language in the agreement usually replaces and supersedes the obligations of any outstanding, earlier Confidentiality Agreement.

B. The Letter of Intent

A buyer and a seller often enter into a Letter of Intent at the conclusion of a successful initial phase of negotiations. The letter, usually prepared

by counsel to the purchaser, identifies the
structure of the contemplated transaction and
summarizes its basic terms, including terms of
payment and the principal conditions to the
closing. These conditions may include, for example,
approvals by government agencies and consents by
third parties, financing arrangements by the purchaser, and achievement of stated net earnings by
the target. The buyer and seller anticipate that a
definitive written acquisition agreement will
follow.

The parties to most Letters of Intent do not
view the letter as establishing binding contractual
rights on the deal itself; it is a moral obligation to
close the deal on the stipulated terms. At the
option of the parties, Letters of Intent can be
binding contracts with open-ended terms—the
strongest contract is an agreement on essential
terms with other terms implicitly agreed to as
whatever is reasonable, based on custom and
practice, e.g., *Iteck Corp. v. Chicago Aerial Ind.,
Inc.* (Del. 1968); the weakest contract is an agreement to bargain in good faith towards a deal. E.g.,
Teachers Ins. & Annuity Assoc. v. Tribune Co.
(N.Y. 1987). Courts are left to determine whether
Letters of Intent are contracts when the parties
are not explicit on their legal effect. The cases are
fact-specific as judges and juries seek to discern
the parties' objective intent; there is much room in
such a trial for effective advocacy. See, e.g., *R.G.
Group, Inc. v. Horn & Hardart Co.* (2d Cir. 1984).
Good lawyers include explicit language on the

legally binding effect of the letter that leaves no room for doubt.

Clients like Letters of Intent, while their lawyers often do not. Both the buyer and seller to an acquisition prefer a preliminary commitment from the other before they incur the substantial costs of negotiating a definitive agreement and performing or allowing to be performed an acquisition review of the selling company. Both parties can see if there are deal-breaking terms and conditions. The letter also helps the buyer in lining up financing and establishes a clear trigger for compliance with regulatory filings (under the Hart-Scott-Rodino Act) and for public announcements.

Lawyers worry that courts will use the letter to give a disgruntled party relief if an anticipated deal does not close. Letters of Intent also affect bargaining leverage. Sellers push buyers into settling key terms in some detail before buyers have access to seller's records and information. Once agreed, the party asking for changes from the terms in the Letters of Intent, usually the buyer, has the burden of justification ("I thought we had a deal."). Once the parties sign a Letter of Intent, however, the bargaining advantage may be with the buyers, as the letters create an expectation of an acquisition on the part of third parties—investors, customers and vendors—that may pressure seller managers to close a deal and accede to buyers' additional demands. In any event, buyers want a "no-shop" commitment and maximum flexibility to change the terms once they learn more about the selling company; sellers want a clear understanding on the price and other key parts of the acquisition agreement, including understandings on employment agreements for retaining desired personnel.

C. The Acquisition Contract

Most acquisition agreements for privately-traded companies follow a basic structure. Section 1 is a glossary of defined terms. Section 2 contains the details of the basic exchange—the stock or assets to be acquired, the consideration to be paid and the timetable for the closing. Usually, Sections 3 and 4 contain the *representations and warranties* of the seller and purchaser, respectively. Following the representations and warranties are two sections on covenants—Section 5 on covenants for the seller and Section 6 on covenants for the purchaser. The next two sections—Sections 7 (for the purchaser) and 8 (for the seller)—contain conditions precedent to the obligations of both parties to execute the exchange at the closing. The next section usually outlines the circumstances in which each party may terminate the deal (Section 9 on termination). This section is followed by a section on indemnification (Section 10) specifying remedies for each party's breach of the agreement. A final section (Section 11) contains miscellaneous provisions.

The major difference between a stock purchase acquisition of a privately-held company and an asset acquisition is in Section 2 on the basic exchange, when the purchaser is buying assets and they must be identified in Section 2 and its accompanying schedules. Moreover, the purchaser's agreement on which liabilities it will assume in an asset deal must be carefully specified. In many asset acquisitions, the purchaser agrees to assume those liabilities ordinary and necessary to the daily operations of the business purchased but does not assume extraordinary or contingent liabilities.

The representations and warranties are statements of fact that exist or will exist at the time of closing. Technically, representations are statements as to existing circumstances and warranties cover future situations. Most lawyers compact the two concepts and refer to them in a run-on term as *reps-and-warranties*. The seller's representations are detailed descriptions about the business being acquired and are much more detailed than the buyer's. The seller's common representations include not only matters routine to all businesses (a representation that the entity is in "good standing" legally, for example) but also extensive provisions on such matters as environmental claims, employee benefits, intellectual property and products liability claims, each of which could result in significant liabilities of the buyer after closing. The buyer's representations deal mainly with a buyer's ability and authority to enter into the acquisition.

Many of the representations refer to a Disclosure Letter that supplements the acquisition agreement. This letter has sections for lists of items that correspond with specified representations. Sometimes the lists give full descriptions. For example, a part of the Disclosure Letter will contain a list of all real property, leaseholds or other interests owned by the seller and a corresponding representation affirming that the list in the Disclosure Letter is complete and accurate and that seller owns, with good and marketable title, all property it purports to own. Other parts of the Disclosure Letter may contain exceptions to a blanket statement in the representations. For example, a representation will state that there are no contracts with relatives of board members other than those listed in the Disclosure Letter and the letter will list a contract between the firm and a mother-in-law. Some parties append schedules to an acquisition agreement, one schedule per representation section, rather than use a Disclosure Letter, but the effect is the same.

The conditions precedent to the obligations of the purchaser and seller specify what must be true for the parties to be bound at the closing to execute the basic exchange (cash for stock, cash for assets, and so on). These provisions detail what each party can expect from the other at the closing. One of the important conditions is a *bring-down* clause in which the seller reaffirms all the representations as accurate as of the closing date. Thus each representation operates (often subject to a materiality condition) as a closing condition. Other conditions include the performance of each of the covenants, all necessary governmental consents, opinions of counsel, and the presentation of the required supplementary documents (an escrow agreement, an employment agreement, a release and an estoppel certificate, for example). In the acquisition of a publicly-traded company the conditions may include *comfort letters* from the SEC on the accounting effect of the transaction and *fairness opinions* from independent investment bankers on the reasonableness of the price.

If a condition of one party is not satisfied, the other party may elect not to close the deal; this condition is a *walk-away right*. Note the difference between conditions and covenants. A breach of a covenant gives remedies under the indemnification section; the failure of a condition justifies a refusal to close. An agreement states explicitly that accuracy of most of the reps-and-warranties at both the time of execution of the agreement and the closing and the satisfaction of most covenants covering obligations due at closing are closing conditions. There are conditions that may not be covenants or reps-and-warranties, however.

Sellers will negotiate for a materiality qualification on many of the conditions. Sellers want purchasers' walk rights contingent on only non-trivial failures of conditions; that is, the purchaser can refuse to close only if there are material inaccuracies in the representations. This can pose a problem if a representation already has a materiality qualifier (a *double materiality* qualification) and drafters have to take care to separately handle representations that already have materiality qualifiers in the condition section. Moreover, most indemnification sections—providing for damages if one party breaches the contract—provide sellers with a *basket* amount (a minimum amount that damages must exceed before the seller owes anything). This deductible recognizes that representations on an ongoing business are unlikely to be perfectly accurate and that the parties do not want disputes over insignificant amounts.

A substantial majority of the indemnification provisions place limits on the right of the buyer to pursue remedies other than those specified in the language of the provision. A majority of agreements also cap the indemnification obligation at 30 to 50 percent of the purchase price. Many agreements include not only general language to the effect that the seller will indemnify the buyer for breaches, but also language specific to indemnification for tax problems and for environmental claims.

The buyers intend the indemnification section to specify and add to otherwise available remedies and to provide that the remedies *survive* the closing. A seller negotiates for an exclusive declaration of remedies and an *as-is* sale—no survival of the remedies after the closing. The survival right is particularly important in light of the intensive legal audit undertaken by the purchaser's representatives. The purchaser may not have discovered a major problem with the seller's business and after closing will want to sue the seller for a false representation. The purchaser's remedies must survive the closing and a court must hold that the purchaser was not at fault somehow for not finding the defect in its acquisition review of the seller's business (that the purchaser did not somehow assume the risk or the like).

The final section of miscellaneous provisions contains those boilerplate provisions taught in first-year contracts courses as necessary. Most of the provisions aid courts in interpreting the basic contract: There are provisions on integration (remember the parol evidence rule?), waiver, severability, section headings, form of notices, time as of the essence, choice of governing law, and so on. There are also a few provisions that add material terms to the deal—the provision on successors and assigns, who pays the deal's expenses, and who may make public announcements about the transaction.

D. Documents That Supplement the Basic Contract

The Employment or Non-Competition Agreement. If the purchaser wants the services of one or more of the employees of the seller, the purchaser may demand an *employment agreement* that binds the employee to stay with the business after the acquisition. The employment agreement will often contain a non-competition clause, discouraging a retained individual from leaving the purchaser's employment after the acquisition. If, on the other hand, the purchaser is not employing seller personnel with access to sensitive business information, the purchaser may demand a *non-competition agreement* to stop employees of the seller from competing with the business once the purchaser takes over. This can be accomplished by a restrictive covenant in the acquisition agreement or by means of a separate agreement.

Courts do not like such agreements and will enforce them only if they are reasonable in geographic scope and duration and are necessary to protect clear business interests in trade secrets and goodwill. E.g., *Wilson v. Electro Marine Systems, Inc.* (7th Cir. 1990) (New York and Illinois law).

The Release. In an acquisition the principle shareholders (and perhaps other agents, employees and officers of the seller) deliver a *release* at the closing. The release usually covers all claims which the releasing parties had, or arising from any matter that existed, as of the closing date against the purchaser and the selling company. Without such a release, for example, if a purchaser asserts claims against individual shareholders of the seller, the individuals might assert that the claims relate to actions taken by them as officers and directors of the seller and present a claim for indemnification against the successor of the seller, the purchaser. The release provides a clean break from the prior owners.

The Non-Negotiable Promissory Note. If the purchaser delivers a promissory note to the sellers at the closing as part of the exchange, the note will contain standard terms, the interest rate, the amortization schedule, the manner of payment, events of default and remedies. The sellers want the promissory note to be negotiable and the buyers want the promissory note to be non-negotiable. If the note is non-negotiable, the seller cannot pass it on to a holder in due course (free from purchaser claims under the acquisition agreement). Moreover, a non-negotiable note is subject to the purchaser's set-off rights for any claims the purchaser may have for breach of the acquisition agreement. See *D'Oench, Duhme & Co. v. FDIC* (U.S. 1947) (set-off rights not effective against holders in due course). As such, the note secures, in a fashion, the obligations of the agreement. Other issues to be resolved include whether the note is secured, the availability of a guarantor, and the priority of the purchaser's obligation relative to the purchaser's other debts. Potential collateral could include the stock or assets received by the purchaser in the acquisition. In a stock acquisition, if the note is secured by the assets of the seller, the transaction generates fraudulent transfer (conveyance) risks.

Documents on Performance Guarantees—an Escrow Agreement. The *escrow agreement* provides for an escrow of funds available to the purchaser to satisfy claims the purchaser may have or develop under the acquisition agreement for matters such as the seller's breach of a representation. Sellers often ask that access to the escrowed funds be the purchaser's exclusive post-closing remedy. Most escrow agreements provide for an institutional escrow agent that dispenses the funds under the terms specified. If the purchaser makes no claims against the funds, they revert to the seller after a specified period of time.

E. Due Diligence Documents

The purchaser's attorneys use an acquisition review checklist to do a thorough legal audit of the seller's business. Many lawyers refer to the audit as *legal due diligence*, a reference from the due diligence investigation conducted by an under-writer's counsel in a public offering of securities. The audit precedes the signing of a final acquisition agreement to help the purchaser accurately price the sellers' business and continues after the signing in preparation for the closing to give the purchaser, at the time of closing, a high level of confidence in the accuracy and completeness of the seller's representations and warranties in the acquisition agreement. The acquisition review begins with an *engagement letter* from the purchaser to its lawyers, specific to the transaction. The lawyers then send a *document request* to the lawyers for the seller asking for copies of documents needed to answer questions on the checklist. The purchaser's lawyers then prepare a *work program*, with deadines, and prepare answers to the questions on a comprehensive checklist.

§ 9.   The Contract for an Acquisition of a Publicly-Traded Company

An acquisition contract for a publicly-traded company is much shorter. The document has very limited seller reps-and-warranties and no post-closing indemnification rights against seller's public shareholders.

The purchaser of a publicly-traded company has the comfort of having access to substantial public information about the seller (all subject to the powerful anti-fraud provisions of the federal securities legislation) and hence does not need a comprehensive set of representations and warranties. The seller will commonly represent that it has made all required filings with the SEC and that the filings comply with the federal securities acts in all material respects. Occasionally, the purchaser will also ask the seller to represent separately that the financial statements in the annual and quarterly reports have been prepared in accordance with GAAP (Generally Accepted Accounting Principles), fairly present the financial condition of the seller, or are correct and complete.

In the acquisition of a publicly-traded company, the consideration will be disbursed to a diffuse group of seller shareholders either on or immediately after the acquisition. Post-closing relief from those shareholders often is not practicable so the acquisition agreement usually does not give the purchaser indemnification rights against the selling company shareholders. The only indemnification section is one that protects the officers and directors of the selling company from liability from claims arising from the transaction.

CHAPTER 3

LITIGATION ON ACQUISITION CONTRACTS

§ 10. One of the Parties to an Executed Contract Refuses to Close

After the parties to an acquisition have executed an acquisition contract, one of the parties may terminate the deal and refuse to close. Most corporate codes provide that an acquisition agreement may provide expressly that a board of directors retains the power unilaterally to abandon a merger before the merger's effective date (usually the closing date) even after any ratifying shareholder vote. E.g., DGCL § 251(d) (mergers and consolidations), § 271(b) (asset sales). The Revised Model Act has an opt-out provision (agreements may be abandoned unless they otherwise provide), in contrast to the opt-in provision in the Delaware code, and also states that an abandonment is subject to the contractual rights of the other party. MBCA § 11.08.

Rather than abandon a deal, some boards prefer to let their shareholders vote a deal down when circumstances surrounding the deal sour. In 1998 the Delaware legislature amended DGCL § 251, governing mergers, to require that the board of directors declare the advisability of a merger agreement before submitting it to the stockholders. The section was also amended to provide that a merger agreement may require that it be sub- mitted to the stockholders even if the board, subse- quent to its initial approval thereof, determines that the agreement is no longer advisable and recommends that the stockholders reject it.

A. The Seller Refuses to Close

The reference in the MBCA to the contractual rights of a frustrated party in an abandoned acqui- sition agreement raises the question of whether a selling firm board can bind itself contractually not to abandon an acquisition and to use its best efforts to obtain an affirmative shareholder vote. If so, the purchaser can successfully sue the selling firm for contract damages even though the selling firm's board has exercised its expressly reserved right to abandon an acquisition agreement. In *Allegheny Energy, Inc. v. DQE, Inc.* (3d Cir. 1999), for example, the Third Circuit was willing to levy more than damages; the court held that it would specifically enforce an acquisition agreement when the contract language in a stock swap merger con- ditioned termination on a material breach of the agreement that could not be cured.

A Second Bidder Offers More Value. The most difficult case for the selling board occurs when a second bidder offering more value appears after the board has signed an acquisition contract with an initial bidder. If the selling board has signed an acquisition contract containing a best efforts clause, what is the import of the clause?

A best efforts clause can be very strict (the board must recommend the deal to shareholders even if a higher offer has been made and may not negotiate or enter into competing contracts with other bidders) or have some leeway (the board must recommend the deal to shareholders if there are no higher offers and the board can neither solicit other offers nor give confidential information to other potential bidders). Most clauses are of the latter ilk and are called *no-shop* clauses. The obligation of a board to be candid with its shareholders means that a strict clause could produce the odd result of a board telling their shareholders of a higher offer and then recommending they accept a lower offer.

At issue is the power of the seller to enter into such contractual provisions. The Ninth Circuit has held that the selling board has such power. *Jewel Cos., Inc. v. PayLess Drug Stores Northwest, Inc.* (9th Cir. 1984). But the Delaware courts seem to view the stronger versions of such a clause (prohibiting the selling firm from considering competing offers, for example) as an inherent breach of the selling board's fiduciary duty. See *ACE Limited v. Capital Re Corp.* (Del. Ch. 1999). See also *Paramount Communications v. QVC Network* (Del. 1994) (*dicta*), citing favorably *ConAgra, Inc. v. Cargill, Inc.* (Neb. 1986).

Many acquisition agreements moot the *Jewel* case problem by including an express *fiduciary out* clause. The provision protects the directors of a target company from having to choose between violating their fiduciary obligation to shareholders and violating a purchase agreement. Under the language of a fiduciary out provision, the directors are excused from any action that would constitute a violation of their fiduciary duty. For example, such a clause would allow a target board to negotiate with a third party despite a no-shop clause or waive the requirement that a board recommend a deal to its shareholders.

Suits Against the Second Bidder. If a court finds that a second bidder induces a selling firm to breach a valid and enforceable contract with an initial bidder, the second bidder is liable to the frustrated first bidder for tort damages. See *Jewel*, supra. One of the largest jury verdicts ever awarded, $10.53 billion, came in such a case. *Texaco, Inc. v. Pennzoil Co.* (Tex. 1988).

Termination Fees. When the buyer has leverage in an acquisition negotiation, it will often insist on including termination fees in the acquisition agreement. A common example is found in the facts of *Brazen v. Bell Atlantic Corp.* (Del. 1997). The parties to a stock swap merger agreement agreed that a party would pay the other $200 million if the party's board terminated the agreement or the party's shareholders refused to ratify the agreement because there was a competing offer for that party. If the competing offer resulted in an acquisition within 18 months of the merger agreement, the terminating party would pay an additional $350 million. The Delaware Supreme Court upheld the clause, using the liquidated damages test from contract law: The damages have to be uncertain and the amount agreed upon has to be reasonable.

B. The Buyer Refuses to Close

If the buyer refuses to tender consideration at the closing, the selling firm has a cause of action for breach. Such cases are rare, but they do exist. In an asset acquisition the answer is straightforward: The selling firm itself sues for traditional contract damages. In aborted stock acquisitions of privately-traded firms, the selling firm shareholders, who would have received the consideration directly from the buyer, are typically signatory parties to the acquisition contract and are therefore the primary plaintiffs on the contract. The firm, through its agents, is also often a signatory to the contract in a stock acquisition and can sue for reliance losses. In aborted tender offers for publicly-traded corporations, tendering shareholders can sue under a contract theory (in addition to claims based on violations of federal securities acts) if the bidder refuses to close when all the tender offer conditions have been met. See, e.g., *In re Gulf Oil/Cities Service Tender Offer Litigation* (N.Y. 1989).

In statutory mergers, the selling firm share-holders would have received the consideration from the buyer but they are often not included on the acquisition contract. The selling firm shareholders must sue on some form of third-party beneficiary theory; the selling firm can sue for reliance damages. In some contracts there is boilerplate language stating that the contract confers no rights on third parties to sue on the contract. In such cases, if a selling firm cannot sue on its shareholders' behalf, the clause limits the damages to the selling firm's reliance expenditures. At least one court has held that under such language the firm cannot sue on behalf of its shareholders. See *In re Gulf*, supra. In the *Cities Service* case, for example, the selling firm recovered greenmail payments spent to clear out a competing bidder and attorney fees spent on the failed deal. *Cities Service Co. v. Gulf Oil Corp.* (Okla. 1999).

§ 11. Nasty Post-Closing Surprises

A. The Buyer Discovers It Has Overpaid

There are numerous cases involving claims by a buyer, who has taken control of a selling firm after closing on an acquisition, that the selling firm is not what it was represented to be. In other words, the buyer overpaid for the selling firm and the overpayment was due to the selling firm's breach of its reps-and-warranties under the acquisition agreement. Many cases revolve around the accuracy of the selling firm's financial statements. See, e.g., *Medcom Holdings Co. v. Baxter Travenol Labs, Inc.* (7th Cir. 1997) (balance sheet overstated asset values).

B. The Selling Firm or the Selling Shareholders Discover They Were Underpaid

Courts usually give short shrift to a selling firm board's claim that it sold too dearly. E.g., *Ontario Teachers' Pension Plan Board v. IG Holdings Inc.* (N.Y. 2000) (pension plan sold stock into a tender offer and later discovered the sale was below market value).

PART II. LEGAL RULES AFFECTING THE CHOICE OF ACQUISITION FORM

CHAPTER 4

SHAREHOLDER VOTING AND APPRAISAL RIGHTS

As was noted in Chapter 2 above, state corporate codes allocate shareholder voting and appraisal rights in acquisitions depending on whether the acquisition is a statutory merger, a sale of substantially all the assets or a stock acquisition. Since a desired end result can often be achieved through more than one transactional form, lawyers have structured transactions to minimize the costs of corporate code shareholder voting and appraisal requirements. Their efforts have two parts. First lawyers pick a state of incorporation, usually Delaware, which gives them planning flexibility. Second, lawyers chose among the state's sections to minimize shareholder voting and appraisal rights.

§ 12. State Statutory Law on Shareholder Voting

Acquisitions for Stock. When the purchasing firm is paying for the target with voting common stock of the purchasing firm (or securities convertible into common shares), shareholder voting rights are the most robust. The general rule in the state statutes is that the shareholders of both the constituent firms have voting rights.

There are five important exceptions. The first two exceptions are found in most states' corporate codes. One, if the amount of common stock in the purchasing firm used in the acquisition is less than 20 percent of its outstanding shares, the purchasing firm shareholders do not vote. E.g., DGCL § 251(f) (statutory mergers; all common included in the calculation); MBCA § 6.21(f) (all acquisitions; only voting common in the calculation); CGCL § 1201(b) (a five-sixths rule for all acquisitions; only voting common included in the calculation). Two, in stock-for-stock acquisitions, the target firm shareholders do not vote. The target shareholder's individual decision on whether or not to tender their shares supplants their need for a collective vote.

Exceptions three through five are found in the Delaware code and the numerous states that follow Delaware's statutes. California and the states that adopt the 1999 revisions to the ABA's Model

Business Corporation Act do not have these exceptions.

Three, if the purchasing firm in an asset acquisition is a Delaware corporation (or incorporated in a state that follows Delaware's statute), the purchasing firm shareholders do not vote. But see MBCA § 6.21(f); CGCL §§ 181(c), 1200(c) & 1201(a). Four, if the purchasing firm in a triangular acquisition is a Delaware corporation (or incorporated in a state that follows Delaware's statute), the purchasing firm shareholders do not vote. In such triangular mergers, the shareholders in the target firm vote but the shareholders in the parent company do not. (The parent board of directors holds and votes the shares of the subsidiary used as an acquisition vehicle in the merger.) But see MBCA § 6.21(f); CGCL §§ 1200(e) & 1201(a). Five, if the purchasing firm in a stock acquisition is a Delaware corporation (or incorporated in a state that follows Delaware's statute), the shareholders in the purchasing firm, as well as those in the target firm, do not have voting rights. But see MBCA § 6.21(f) (purchasing firm shareholders vote); CGCL §§ 181(b), 1200(b) & 1201(a) (same).

Acquisitions for Cash or Cash Equivalents. When the purchasing firm is paying cash or cash equivalents—non-voting, non-convertible stock or non-convertible debt—for the target, shareholders have more limited voting rights. (In Delaware the category would not include non-voting common stock.) In asset acquisitions (cash-for-assets), the

shareholders in the target vote, but the shareholders in the purchasing firm do not. DGCL § 271;
MBCA § 12.01. In cash mergers, the shareholders
of the target vote, but those in the purchasing
corporation do not, if and only if the target merges
into the purchasing corporation and there is no
change to the rights and privileges of the shares
held by the shareholders of the purchasing company. DGCL § 251(f); MBCA § 11.04(g). In stock
acquisitions (cash-for-stock), the shareholders of
neither constituent corporation have voting rights.

*"Reverse Acquisitions": Allocating the Vote in
Delaware Corporations.* The differences in voting
rights among the various types of acquisitions
empower lawyers not only to minimize voting
rights but also to allocate them among the
constituent parties. The choice of a cash-for-assets
acquisition, for example, eliminates the voting
rights of the shareholders of the purchasing firm.
By doing a *reverse acquisition*, that is, having the
actual target firm technically purchase the assets
of the actual purchasing firm, planners can
allocate the voting rights to shareholders in the
purchasing firm and eliminate the voting right in
the target. In Diagram 4 in Chapter 1 above,
assume that A Corp is the target and B Corp is the
purchasing corporation. In the stock-for-assets
reverse acquisition, the A Corp stock transferred to
B Corp constitutes over 51 percent of the A Corp
voting stock outstanding after the acquisition.
Planners thus transfer control of A Corp to B Corp
and then dissolve B Corp, distributing the con-

trolling block of A Corp voting stock through to the original B Corp shareholders. Under Delaware statutes the shareholders of B Corp vote and the shareholders of A Corp do not. Under California statutes and the 1999 revision to the Model Business Corporation Act, however, A Corp shareholders do have the right to vote. MBCA § 6.21(f); CGCL §§ 181(c), 1200(c) & 1201(a).

§ 13. State Statutory Law on Shareholder Appraisal Rights for Dissenting Shareholders

Shareholders who have the right to vote on acquisitions or recapitalizations usually have, by state statute, *dissenters' rights*. Dissenters' rights are also known as *appraisal rights* or *buy-out rights*. All states give shareholders who dissent to certain types of acquisitions a right to petition a state court for the fair cash value of their shares.

If a substantial minority block of shareholders demands cash in these proceedings, known as appraisal proceedings, and the constituent firms in a stock swap acquisition are cash poor, the mere notice by the dissenting shareholders that they might assert their appraisal rights can terminate the acquisition. Many acquisition agreements in stock swap deals expressly condition a closing on the absence of even a small percentage (three percent or more) of target shareholders claiming dissenters' rights. Moreover, in all types of acquisitions it can be very embarrassing to a board of directors if a state judge gives a dissenting share-holder more money than the board negotiated for shareholders that supported the acquisition. Supporting shareholders may turn and sue the board for a breach of its fiduciary duty.

There are four central issues in the basic definition of the appraisal remedy: First, what kinds of transactions support the right; second, what the procedural requirements are for perfecting the right; third, how courts determine fair value; and fourth, whether the right is the exclusive remedy for dissenting shareholders.

A. The Scope of the Appraisal Remedy

Under the Delaware corporate code, the general rule is that dissenting shareholders in statutory mergers, including short-form mergers in which the minority shareholders do not have a right to vote, have appraisal rights. DGCL § 262. The Delaware section is one of the more limited of all such provisions in state corporate codes, however. First, the Delaware provision applies only to mergers; it does not apply in asset sales under § 271, nor to amendments to the certificate of incorporation under § 242. Delaware, as do all other states, gives non-voting shareholders in short-form mergers appraisal rights. (In short-form mergers a partially-owned subsidiary merges into its parent and the parent owns over 90 percent of the subsidiary's stock.) Second, the Delaware provision has an exception for securities of publicly-traded corporations, the *market-out exception.*

Most other states more closely link voting rights and appraisal rights in acquisitions. For example, most states provide appraisal rights to the shareholders of the selling firm in an asset sale, and almost half the states give appraisal rights to dissenting shareholders when certain amendments to the articles of incorporation are approved. There are exceptions. Some states grant appraisal rights when shareholders have no voting rights. Michigan and South Carolina, for example, grant dissenters' rights to shareholders of a corporation after an acquisition of a controlling block of the shares.

On the other hand, some states refuse appraisal rights to shareholders who do have voting rights. The best-known example, noted above, is Delaware's refusal to give appraisal rights to voting shareholders in asset acquisitions. Other states have more limited exceptions. The New York business corporation law and the 1984 version of the ALI-ABA Revised Model Business Corporations Act give appraisal rights to shareholders of corporations selling substantially all their assets for stock in the purchasing corporation but not to shareholders of corporations selling substantially all their assets for cash if the selling firm dissolves within a year of the sale. NYCLA § 910(a)(B); MBCA § 13.02(a)(3) (1984). California provides appraisal rights to selling firm shareholders in stock-for-assets acquisitions but not cash-for-assets acquisitions, regardless of whether the selling firm dissolves. CGCL § 1300 (omitting reference to § 1001 transactions). The drafters argue that appraisal rights ought to apply only when shareholders receiving stock are forced to become shareholders in a different corporation.

As noted above, appraisal rights are controversial. The 1984 version of the ALI-ABA Revised Model Business Corporation Act contains a chapter on appraisal rights that is one of the most liberal grants of appraisal rights in the history of state corporate codes. In a complete reversal of approach, the Committee on Corporate Laws recommended in 1999 that states adopt a new chapter that substantially reduces the scope of the chapter that had been in place since 1984. Some states may choose to keep the 1984 version; others may adopt the 1999 model. The 1999 version competes with Delaware for the title of most conservative state provision.

The 1999 version of the MBCA de-links shareholder voting and appraisal rights in several important contexts and, thereby, eliminates appraisal rights in several instances in which it would have been available under the 1984 provisions. First, shareholders entitled to vote on an acquisition are not entitled to appraisal rights if the transactions would not alter the terms of the securities that they hold. Shareholders of the surviving corporation in a merger, for example, even if voting on the acquisition (because the firm issues a new block of stock that exceeds 20 percent of the stock outstanding), do not have appraisal rights if their shares remain outstanding after the merger and the rights and privileges of their shares remain the same. This exception is not found in Delaware. Second, the new chapter eliminates appraisal rights on amendments to the articles of incorporation unless the amendment effects a reverse stock split. Third, the new chapter includes a market-out exception that was not in the 1984 provisions. The market-out exception is not as broad as the Delaware exception, however; it does not apply in conflict-of-interest transactions. A conflict of interest exists when the senior managers or the controlling shareholders have interests in both parties in an acquisition. The market exemption is not lost, however, if senior management receives specified financial benefits from employment, consulting, or severance contracts as a result of the transaction. The 1999 revision does provide appraisal rights in one context that the 1984 version did not. Under the new chapter, shareholders in a cash-for-assets acquisition have appraisal rights. And fourth, a corporation may amend its certificate of incorporation to eliminate appraisal rights for preferred shareholders (with a delayed effective date of one year).

B. Appraisal Procedures

The appraisal procedures (both the 1984 and 1999 versions) in the MBCA are significantly different from the procedures in Delaware's corporate code. The Model Act seeks to readjust the balance between the corporation and the dissenting stockholders in favor of shareholders. The principal changes are aimed, first, at eliminating much of the delay in getting funds into the hands of dissenting shareholders; second, at forcing corporations to take more initiative in settling the claims; and, third, at shifting more of the expenses of the procedure to the corporation.

Under Delaware law, a corporation contemplating a transaction that gives rise to shareholder appraisal rights must notify shareholders of these rights 20 days before the corporation submits the transaction to shareholders for approval. Then each dissenting shareholder demanding appraisal rights must so notify the corporation before the vote on the transaction. If shareholders ratify the transaction, the corporation must notify dissenting shareholders (who gave proper notice) that appraisal rights are available. This second corporate notification must occur within 10 days of the transaction's effective date. The shareholder must then, within 20 days of the second notice, demand from the corporation appraisal of his shares. If the shareholder is unsatisfied, he must, within 120 days of the transaction's effective date, file a petition in the court of

chancery demanding a determination of the value
of his stock. A trial on the petition can take several
years. As a result of this lengthy process, the
dissatisfied stockholder may not receive money for
her shares for quite some time.

The MBCA, on the other hand, stresses the
importance of getting some cash value in the
dissenting shareholders' hands quickly. Under
Chapter 13 of the Model Act, corporations, in their
notice of a shareholder meeting, must inform
shareholders of their appraisal rights. Dissenting
shareholders must give the corporation a written
notice before the pivotal shareholder meeting of
their intent to demand payment. Once the transaction is approved, the corporation must, within 10
days, notify the dissenting shareholders of the
maturation of their appraisal rights and send them
a specified form. If the dissenting shareholder
returns the form within 40 days and demands payment, the corporation must pay that shareholder,
within 30 days, cash equal to the *corporation's* estimated fair value for the shares. If the dissenting
shareholder is dissatisfied with the amount, he
may, within 30 days of payment, inform the corporation of his *own* estimate. If the corporation fails
to settle the discrepancy, the corporation must
commence a proceeding within 60 days of the
shareholder's demand to determine the fair value
of the shares. If the corporation fails to settle or
sue, it must pay the shareholder his demand. The
effect of the Model Act's procedure is to place some
cash in the hands of dissenters soon after the

meeting and to place the obligation to petition a court on the corporation rather than the dissenting shareholder.

Delaware Code § 262(j) does not provide for the shifting of attorney and expert fees and expenses to the corporation. The fees and expense may be charged pro rata against the value of all the shares represented in the appraisal proceeding. Thus, for shareholders to assess whether an appraisal action in Delaware would be profitable, they must net out the potential expenses of attorneys and experts that can run into six figures. The Model Business Corporation Act allows courts to shift such expenses to the corporation. MBCA § 13.31(b)-(d).

C. Case Law on Fair Value in Appraisal Proceedings

The fair value issue in appraisal proceedings has two separate components. First, judges, often befuddled by competing financial experts, must value the shares in issue. In *Weinberger v. UOP* (Del. 1983), the Delaware Supreme Court held that this included "proof of value by any techniques or methods which are generally considered acceptable in the financial community and otherwise admissible in court." The valuation is of the company apportioned pro rata among the shareholders. The courts refuse to attach a minority discount to non-controlling shares. See *Cavalier Oil Corp. v. Harnett* (Del. 1989). Expert witnesses calculate value based on prior stock trades, discounted cash flow and comparisons with comparable companies.

Second, if the legislation is not specific, judges must address the bottomless policy question of whether dissenting shareholders should participate in the gains from the acquisition and, if so, how to measure those gains. The issue of whether and how to account for the potential gains of the merger or acquisition divides states. Should shareholders receive the value of their shares before the announcement of the merger affects share price, or should shareholders claim a portion of the gains generated by the merger itself? Sometimes the question is put in terms of whether the shareholders should receive a part of the "control premium" in acquisitions that involve a change of control. Occasionally the question is explicitly resolved by statute. More often the matter is left to the judiciary.

The Delaware statutes direct the courts to

appraise the shares, determining their fair value exclusive of any element of value arising from the accomplishment or expectation of the merger, together with a fair rate of interest, if any, to be paid upon the amount determined to be the *fair* value. In determining such fair value, the Court shall take into account all relevant factors....

DGCL § 262(h). In *Weinberger*, the Delaware Supreme Court held that "[o]nly the speculative elements of value that may arise from the 'accomplishment or expectation' of the merger are excluded." Elements of future value, including the nature of the enterprise, which are known or susceptible of proof as of the date of the merger and not the product of speculation, may be considered.

A few other states have attempted to resolve the issues by establishing a valuation date. States that do not want to include acquisition value in the appraisal award require that a court value the corporation on the eve of the shareholder vote and that the valuation exclude any premium for the deal itself. NJSA § 14A:11-3; ORCA § 1701.85(C). On the other hand, a few states expressly include acquisition value in the statutory language. New York is an example of a state legislature that bit the bullet on valuing the potential of the transaction itself. NYCLA § 623(h)(4). The ALI-ABA Revised Model Business Corporation Act is moving towards the New York position.

In the 1984 version of the MBCA, fair value is determined "immediately before the effectuation of the corporate action to which the dissenter objects, excluding any appreciation or depreciation in anticipation of the corporate action unless exclusion would be inequitable." RMBCA § 13.01(3) (1984). The 1999 proposed amendment to the section deletes the final dependent clause of the 1984 version and invites the court to use "customary and current valuation concepts and techniques generally employed for similar business in the context of the transaction requiring appraisal." The Official Comment to the 1999 version notes that the language "permits consideration of changes in market price of the corporation's shares in anticipation of the transaction, to the extent the changes are relevant." Yet the Comment also draws a distinction between market value and value attributable to the unique plans of the purchaser. The former is acceptable, the latter is not. The drafters, in essence, respect the claim of a dissenting shareholder that the firm could be sold for a higher price to someone else but do not respect the claim that the managers could have negotiated for a higher price from the actual purchaser.

Cases in Delaware seem to agree with the 1999 version of the Revised Model Business Corporation Act. Acquisition-specific elements of value are not to be included, but adjustments to counter built-in minority discounts are, although the position is not free from considerable doubt. See *MPM Enterprises v. Gilbert* (Del. 1999). How does one estimate the latter and exclude the former? The use of simple comparable company acquisition premiums may overcompensate shareholders; each comparable transaction price includes consideration of elements of synergy value from that specific transaction. The amount of the synergy value reflected in the purchase price of the comparable acquisition depends on the bargaining prowess of the two parties.

D. The Exclusivity of the Appraisal Remedy

The state courts have also struggled with the relationship of the special appraisal remedy procedure to run-of-the-mill derivative litigation based on allegations of breaches of fiduciary duty. Companies want the appraisal remedy to be the exclusive remedy for shareholders complaining about mergers or other covered transactions. Shareholder plaintiffs would prefer to add appraisal proceedings to their pre-existing arsenal of remedies for attacking mergers—breach of fiduciary duty, securities violations and fraud. Neither side has gotten its way. Delaware courts allow shareholders to file additional requests for relief if they uncover evidence in the course of discovery of the pending appraisal case to support claims beyond those of garden-variety fiduciary breaches. *Cede & Co. v. Technicolor* (Del. 1988). See also *Weinberger* (appraisal remedy not adequate "where fraud, misrepresentation, self-dealing, deliberate waste of corporate assets, or gross or palpable overreaching are involved"). The remedy in the non-appraisal proceedings attacking a merger is limited to injunctive relief and rescissory damages, damages that put the shareholders in the same financial position they would have occupied had the transaction not taken place. The Model Business Corporation Act, purporting to follow Delaware law, limits a dissenting shareholder to its appraisal remedy unless "the action is unlawful or fraudulent with respect to the shareholder or the corporation." RMBCA § 13.02(b).

§ 14. State Case Law on Acquisition Form— The De Facto Merger Doctrine and the Business Purpose Doctrine

A. The De Facto Merger Doctrine

The advantage of a stock-for-assets acquisition or a stock-for-stock acquisition over a stock swap statutory merger is that, in all but a few states, the shareholders in the purchasing corporation do not have the right to vote on the transaction nor the right to an appraisal. The states that give shareholders in the purchasing firm voting rights, based on the voting power of the stock issued for use as consideration, are, as noted above, California, New Jersey, Ohio, and Rhode Island. See MBCA § 6.21 (1999 rev.). Purchasing firm shareholders who are angry at not having voting and appraisal rights in such transactions have through the years occasionally taken the matter to court, asking judges to reclassify stock-for-asset transactions or stock-for-stock acquisitions as *de facto* (in reality) statutory mergers. Shareholders ask judges to reclassify the acquisition as a statutory merger and give shareholders their voting and appraisal rights as if the acquisition were a statutory merger. With infrequent and largely discredited exceptions, the shareholders have lost. See *Heilbrunn v. Sun Chemical Corp.* (Del. 1959).

As noted above, shareholders in Delaware corporations do not have appraisal rights if their corporation is the target in an asset acquisition. Shareholders in such acquisitions have complained, arguing that they have been deprived of their appraisal rights through transaction manipulation. The Delaware Supreme Court rejected their *de facto* merger arguments in *Hariton v. Arco Electronic* (Del. 1963):

> We now hold that the reorganization here accomplished through § 271 and a mandatory plan of dissolution and distribution is legal. This is so because the sale-of-assets statute and the merger statute are independent of each other. They are, so to speak, of equal dignity, and the framers of a reorganization plan may resort to either type of corporate mechanics to achieve the desired end.

Courts have also applied the "equal dignity" rule to reject the voting claims of shareholders of the parent in a triangular acquisition (see Diagram 9 in Chapter One), *Equity Group Holdings v. DMG, Inc.* (Fla. 1983), and to reject the voting claims of shareholders of the purchasing corporation in a stock acquisition (see Diagram 7, Step One, in Chapter One). *Irving Bank Corp. v. Bank of New York Co., Inc.* (N.Y. 1988).

There have been a few courts—a very few— that have found for the plaintiff shareholders under a de facto merger theory. E.g., *Rath v. Rath*

Packing Co. (Iowa 1965); *Farris v. Glen Alden Corp.* (Pa. 1958); *Applestein v. United Board & Carton Corp.* (N.J. 1960).

The Iowa and Pennsylvania legislatures subsequently repudiated *Rath* and *Farris* in amendments to the states' corporate codes. The Iowa legislature later rescinded the express rejection of *Rath* on the theory that the new corporation code voting requirements made a *Rath* fact situation impossible. The Pennsylvania legislature's rejection of *Farris* is found in PCSA § 1904 (Purdon 1997). *Applestein* is the lone example of a successful and unrepudiated application of the de facto merger doctrine to shareholder voting claims. NJSA § 14A:10-12 (1998 Supp.) (codifying the case). In Chapter 5 we will see that the de facto merger doctrine has considerably more life when target firm *creditors* are the plaintiffs.

Shareholders can create voting rights in triangular acquisitions or asset acquisitions with express provisions in a corporation's certificate of incorporation, however. *Pasternak v. Glazer* (Del. Ch. 1996) (certificate of incorporation protects the voting rights of the shareholders of the purchasing corporation in a triangular acquisition).

B. Involuntary Squeeze-Outs of Minority Shareholders

In a *cash-out transaction*, the purchasing firm does not want the shareholders of the selling firm to end up holding voting common stock in the purchasing firm. The purchasing firm wants to pay cash for the selling firm's assets or, if cash is not available, to pay the selling firm shareholders in non-voting investments in the purchasing firm—debentures (debt) or non-voting preferred or common stock (equity). The traditional methods are Diagram 3 in Chapter One, the cash-for-assets acquisition, or Diagram 5 in Chapter One, the cash-for-stock acquisition.

A cash-out is also possible using a statutory merger procedure. For a *cash-out statutory merger*, start with Diagram 1 and replace the A Corp shares going to the B Corp shareholders with cash. See Diagram 2. The end result is identical to the post-transaction position in Diagram 3, the cash-for-assets transaction.

Planners often use cash merger transactions to eliminate minority shareholders. The minority block is often a group of residual shareholders that did not tender their shares in a stock acquisition (see Diagram 7, Stage One, in Chapter One). The transactions are known as *squeeze-outs* (or, less frequently, as *freeze-outs*). In a typical squeeze-out, a corporation holding shares in a partially-owned subsidiary drops down a new wholly-owned shell subsidiary and merges the partially-owned sub into the wholly-owned sub (see Diagram 7, Stage Two). The firm gives the minority shareholders in the partially-owned subsidiary cash or debt securities (debentures) for the cancelled shares.

In another, more notorious type of squeeze-out, a corporation with a minority block of shareholders drops down a new wholly-owned shell subsidiary and merges itself into the subsidiary (see Diagram 8 in Chapter One). All the stock in the corporation is cancelled. The majority shareholders in the original firm receive stock in the surviving firm and the minority shareholders receive cash or debt securities.

Minority shareholders, who are expelled against their wishes in both types of squeeze-outs, claim foul. For a short time, the Delaware Supreme Court asked corporations to prove a legitimate business purpose in cash-out mergers. *Singer v. Magnavox Co.* (Del. 1977). The court later overturned the decision, finding it unworkable, and held that merger provisions in corporate codes do authorize such transactions, subject to shareholder claims for fraud or other forms of overreaching. E.g., *Weinberger v. UOP, Inc.* (Del. 1983) (a cash-out merger between a parent and its partially-owned subsidiary). *Singer* may still be followed in other jurisdictions, however. E.g., *Coggins v. New England Patriots Football Club* (Mass. 1986).

A related problem occurs when a firm uses a squeeze-out merger to eliminate its preferred shareholders. In cash-out merger transactions, preferred shareholders who receive cash for their shares have been surprised by the ease with which firms avoid dividend or liquidation preferences or redemption rights attached to their shares. The corporation drops down a wholly-owned subsidiary and merges into the subsidiary, exchanging the stock of the subsidiary for the outstanding stock of the corporation. Preferred shares are exchanged for cash, debt or common shares.

The preferred shareholders, who hold non-voting stock, can lose their shares without a right to vote on the cash-out merger. The class voting provisions of DGCL § 242 on statutory recapital-izations (amendments to the certificate of incorpo-ration require a majority vote of all affected classes of stock) and the absence of class voting provisions in DGCL § 251 on statutory mergers cause lawyers to use statutory mergers to avoid class voting. Preferred shareholders who do not have class voting rights in the merger have asked judges to block such acquisitions. The courts have refused to do so. See *Federal United Corporation v. Havender* (Del. 1940). Courts have also refuse to construe the general privileges on preferred shares as having been triggered by a squeeze-out merger. See *Rauch v. RCA Corp.* (2d Cir. 1988) (preferred share-holders lost claim for redemption price); *Rothschild Int'l Corp. v. Liggett Group* (Del. 1984) (preferred shareholders lost claim for liquidation preference).

Preferred shareholders who wish to protect the special privileges of their shares in cash-out mergers can do so with express language in their investment contracts, embodied in their firm's certificate of incorporation. E.g., *Warner Communi-cations, Inc. v. Chris-Craft Indus., Inc.* (Del. 1989).

§ 15. Stock Exchange Rules on Shareholder Voting

A. Introduction to Stock Exchange Listing Requirements

Our stock markets consist of buyers and sellers of securities trading at mutually agreeable prices. Markets that are deep (have many participants), liquid (have substantial trading volume at any one time), efficient (trading expenses are minimized) and honest (free of manipulation and fraud) are a national treasure. A healthy secondary trading market means firms can raise money to capitalize their businesses at lower cost, stock prices act as guideposts to optimal allocations of capital and other investment, and small investors participate in the trading. The markets also provide employment for banks, institutional investors, broker-dealers, accountants, and lawyers—professionals that service the trading markets.

For the past several decades our stock markets have consisted of three national exchanges: the New York Stock Exchange (NYSE) and the much smaller Amex and Chicago Board Options Exchange (CBOE); five regional stock exchanges (Boston, Philadelphia, Chicago, Pacific and Cincinnati); and our over-the-counter, broker-dealer market (NASDAQ is its largest component). On all the exchanges but one (Cincinnati), stock changes hands on a physical trading floor. On the NASDAQ, dealers post quotations on computer screens and then receive orders via computer link or over the telephone.

The new kids on the block are privately-owned, electronic trading systems (ECNs). These fully-automated systems, still very young, now handle over one and one-half times the trading volume of the Amex and all the regional exchanges combined. The more than 10 electronic trading systems service mostly institutional investors who are dissatisfied with the trading costs and time lags in our traditional markets. A few of the new electronic systems are doing so well that they soon could become viable substitutes for our registered exchanges or NASDAQ.

Our national stock exchanges are private trade organizations of licensed broker/dealers. Most are non-profit corporations with restricted membership. Membership requirements include mastery of basic skills and knowledge, a minimal level of capital, and a reputation for trustworthiness. The members meet and trade securities listed by the exchange. Each exchange has listing requirements for firms traded on the exchange and firms agree to those requirements in a listing contract signed with the exchange. Penalties for violating a listing contract include suspension of trading in and de-listing of the firm's securities.

An exchange designs listing requirements to attract traders: Firms that meet an exchange's listing requirements are, in theory, more attractive to traders than firms that do not. In signing a listing contract, firms promise, among other things, to maintain a minimum float in their securities, to respect conditions on corporate actions that affect outstanding securities, and to be candid and truthful about firm affairs.

Exchanges and other organized trading markets, such as NASDAQ, provide substantial benefits and some problems. On the plus side of the ledger, exchanges have strong incentives to provide rules and enforcement mechanisms that increase investors' returns, and thereby increase investors' demand for listed securities. An exchange has an incentive to create listing rules that are neither too harsh nor too lenient. If the exchange listing requirements are too harsh, firms may view listing as imposing too many costs for the benefit of a listing and choose to list elsewhere. There will be too few securities to trade. If the listing requirements are too lenient, too many firms may engage in acts that defraud or otherwise disadvantage investors and traders will not have confidence in the *bona fides* of the firms listed. In an important sense, the listing requirements and how and whether they are enforced are an important part of the public image of any exchange. Under the Securities and Exchange Act of 1934, exchanges must register with the Securities and Exchange Commission (SEC) and the SEC has oversight responsibility for exchange rules and proceedings. The Act classifies stock exchanges as "Self-Regulatory Organizations" (SROs). They have their own operating rules and structure, and they control their membership with admission and disciplinary rules. Congress has granted the SEC power to oversee SRO operations, to approve all SRO rules and regulations, and, in a rarely-used power, to write SRO rules itself.

B. The NYSE Listing Requirements on Shareholder Voting in Acquisitions

Shareholder approval is required prior to the issuance of common stock, or of securities convertible into or exercisable for common stock, in any transaction, if the common stock has or will have upon issuance voting power equal to or in excess of 20 percent of the voting power outstanding before the issuance of such stock or securities convertible into or exercisable for common stock or if the number of shares of common stock to be issued is or will be equal to or in excess of 20 percent of the number of shares of common stock outstanding before the issuance of the stock. NYSE Listed Company Manual ¶ 312.03. The American Stock Exchange (Amex) and the National Association of Securities Dealers Automatic Quotation System (NASDAQ) have similar rules. Amex Listing Company Manual § 712; NASD Manual—The NASDAQ Stock Market, Rule 4310(c)(25)(H). Note that technically the exchange does not require the vote, but rather a firm's certificate of incorporation, written to comply with exchange listing requirements, compels the vote.

The voting majority required in the NYSE Listing Company Manual is different than the voting majority required by most state corporate codes. The Manual requires only a majority vote of all shares represented or present at the shareholder meeting, provided at least 50 percent of the firm's shares are voted. State corporate codes on acquisitions, if applicable, require, on the other hand, a majority vote of all *outstanding* shares entitled to vote. If there are 1,000 voting shares, under the NYSE listing rules 51 percent of 50 percent of the voting shares (shareholders holding 251 shares) may, in theory, be sufficient for passage. State corporate codes require an affirmative vote of shareholders holding at least 501 shares.

The NYSE also has a special shareholder voting rule for acquisitions in which a senior officer of the acquiring company has a substantial stake in the acquired company, *conflict-of-interest acquisitions*. If a corporation uses over 1 percent in number of its shares or uses shares with over 1 percent in voting power outstanding before the acquisition as consideration in an acquisition, and a director, officer or substantial security holder in the purchasing company has a substantial direct or indirect interest in the target, shareholders of the purchasing company must ratify the transactions. NYSE Listed Company Manual § 312.03(b). NASDAQ requires a vote in conflict-of-interest acquisitions if the consideration offered represents 5 percent or more of the outstanding shares of the purchaser in either number or voting power. NASD

Manual—The NASDAQ Stock Market, Rule 4310(c)(25)(H)(I)(c).

CHAPTER 5

SUCCESSORSHIP ISSUES: ASSIGNMENTS OF CONTRACT RIGHTS AND SUCCESSOR LIABILITY

In corporate law, successorship issues depend on the form of the transaction. State corporate law codes provide that, when two firms merge, the surviving firm (or the new firm) succeeds to the assets and liabilities of the merged firm or firms automatically, as a matter of law. DGCL § 259; MBCA § 11.07. A similar but distinct rule applies to sales of stock. When a firm is acquired through the acquisition of its stock, the firm automatically retains all prior assets and liabilities because the corporation has an independent legal existence. In contrast, when the successor firm acquires some or all of the assets of the predecessor firm, the general rule is that the successor does not assume any liabilities nor take any assets, except as specifically negotiated.

§ 16. Assignments of Licenses, Leaseholds and Other Valuable Contract Rights

If the target in an acquisition has valuable contract rights, at issue is whether the contracts will transfer in the acquisition. Some of the contracts are silent, some have general anti-assignment clauses and others have clauses specific to acquisitions, so-called *control change* clauses. Control change clauses present the easiest case; the terms of the clause control the effect of the acquisition on the contract. Most such clauses stop all transfers of the contract right in all forms of acquisitions without the prior written consent of an opposite party. The more difficult cases are presented by contracts that are silent or have general anti-assignment clauses.

A. Asset Acquisitions

In asset acquisitions each asset is individually transferred by agreement from the target to the purchasing firm. One of the disadvantages of an asset acquisition is that the lawyers must transfer title of all assets—re-deed land, re-title vehicles and so on. Contracts that are silent on assignment do not transfer without the consent of an opposite party if the contracts are personal (contracts for personal services, for example); contracts that are not personal (leases) transfer without the consent of an opposite party. Contracts that are not personal (leases) with general anti-assignment (or anti-transfer) clauses also do not transfer without the consent of an opposite party.

B. Statutory Mergers

All state codes have specific statutes on the effect of a statutory merger on the preexisting rights and obligations of the constituent parties. DGCL §§ 259 & 261. As a general matter, the statutes contain language directing that all rights and obligations of the constituent parties pass to the surviving entity in a statutory merger as a matter of law. Courts have held that the merger statutes override most contracts that are implicitly or expressly non-assignable or non-transferable. In other words, if a target firm holds non-assignable contracts, it can merge into a purchasing firm and the purchasing firm can claim rights under the contracts. For example, a non-assignable lease will transfer in a statutory acquisition.

There is a significant exception, however. The Sixth Circuit has held that, because patent rights are creatures of federal and not state law, federal law on patent licenses overrides the effect-of-merger provisions in state corporate codes. *PPG Industries, Inc. v. Guardian Industries Corp.* (U.S. 1979). Patent licenses do not transfer as a matter of law in mergers. Since patent licenses are "personal," only those licenses with express provisions permitting assignment or transfer will transfer in statutory mergers.

C. Stock Acquisitions

Stock acquisitions, transferring control of a corporation through the transfer of its ownership investment contracts, do not affect contracts of the corporation unless the contract is explicit on the matter. Thus contracts that are silent or have general anti-assignment clauses remain in force through the acquisition. General anti-assignment clauses stop legal assignments or transfers of the contract itself and there has been no such transfer or assignment in a stock acquisition. E.g., *Branmar Theatre Co. v. Branmar* (Del. 1970). Only contracts that have control change clauses that protect specifically against stock ownership changes apply to stock acquisitions.

§ 17. State Law on Successor Liability

In statutory mergers the liabilities of the disappearing corporation reattach to the survivor. In stock acquisitions, the liabilities of the target remain with the target; only ownership of the target changes.

In asset acquisitions, the problem cases occur when a purchaser elects *not* to assume the liabilities of the seller in the acquisition. The seller accepts compensation for its assets and applies the compensation against its liabilities when it dissolves. Creditors who do not get paid before dissolution or whose claims arise after dissolution have limited remedies under corporate codes and fraudulent conveyance statutes. Dissatisfaction with these remedies has led frustrated creditors to claim against the purchaser of the assets under the doctrine of *successor liability*, arguing that the decoupling of the assets and the liabilities was inequitable. The most sympathetic claimants are those *long-tail* or *contingent* claimants whose

injuries do not occur until long after the acquisition and the dissolution of the seller; products
liability claimants are a high profile subgroup.

The general rule on successor liability in asset
acquisitions has always been subject to exceptions
under a common-law, four-part test and, in recent
years, several new exceptions have emerged in the
case law. Some of the new exceptions are in state
law—the most important are in California and
Michigan (each state has a follower or two)—and
some are in federal law developed by federal courts
struggling to apply open-ended federal statutes.
States fall into two camps on successor liability.
The larger camp, represented by Illinois, follows
the traditional rule of four exceptions. The smaller
camp, represented by California, Michigan and
New Jersey, takes a more aggressive stance in
favor of the creditors.

The common-law four-part test for successor
liability in asset acquisitions is that the purchasing corporation assumes the seller's liabilities
when: (1) it expressly agrees to assume them; (2)
the asset sale amounts to a de facto merger; (3) the
purchaser is a mere continuation of the seller; (4)
the sale is for the fraudulent purpose of escaping
liability for the seller's obligations. E.g., *Ruiz v.
Blentech Corporation* (7th Cir. 1996).

In most states, the de facto merger exception
and the mere continuity exception operate in much
the same fashion. The owners of the selling firm

must take stock in the surviving firm. In the mere continuity exception, the owners of the selling firm are the only owners of the purchasing firm. In both exceptions, the purchasing firm must continue the essential operating business of the selling firm in much the same form. Finally, the selling firm must dissolve or otherwise have no assets.

Michigan has expanded and renamed the de facto merger exception, however. Its *continuity-of-enterprise* exception relaxes the requirement that the selling firm owners take stock in the purchasing firm. *Turner v. Bituminous Casualty Co.* (Mich. 1976).

California adopts a fifth exception, the *products line* exception. *Ray v. Alad Corp.* (Cal. 1977). See also *Ramirez v. Amsted Industries* (N.J. 1981). The California products line exception provides that a corporation that purchases a manufacturing business and continues to produce the seller's line of products assumes strict liability in tort for defects in units of the same product line previously manufactured and distributed by the seller. The exception applies in cases involving tort claims where: (1) the plaintiff lacks an adequate remedy against the seller/manufacturer; (2) the purchaser knows about product risks associated with the line of products that it continues; and (3) the seller transfers goodwill associated with the product line.

Wary purchasers use a combination of strategies to minimize nasty surprises—unpriced, unwittingly absorbed liabilities from asset acquisitions. First, purchasers conduct a thorough due diligence investigation of the seller's business, liabilities and insurance before the closing. Second, purchasers insist on several specialized provisions in the acquisition agreement. The purchaser agrees to assume only specifically identified liabilities and secures a comprehensive and thorough set of specific warranties from the seller warranting that there are no other outstanding problems that could lead to additional liabilities. There are, among others, specific warranties on litigation, labor disputes, products liability and environmental claims. The warranties are backed by an indemnification clause from the seller and, if possible, from the seller's shareholders. The seller secures the indemnification obligation by funding an escrow account or by providing a bond or some other form of purchaser insurance. Third, the purchaser uses a triangular acquisition to place the new assets in a wholly-owned subsidiary. Fourth, to the extent possible in light of business imperatives, the purchaser minimizes the appearance of business continuity, avoiding factors that might lead a court to impose successor liability. And fifth, the purchaser requires the seller to maintain its separate corporate existence and its own liability insurance for a specific time following the sale (this is not practical in a tax-free reorganization).

§ 18. Federal Law on Successor Liability

In 1973, the United States Supreme Court fashioned a special rule of successor liability for unfair labor practice claims brought under the National Labor Relations Act. *Golden State Bottling Co. v. NLRB* (U.S. 1973). If a new employer has acquired substantial assets of its predecessor and continued without interruption or substantial change the predecessor's business operations, those employees who have been retained and who have claims against the predecessor can reassert their old claims against the new employer. The successor must have notice of the old claims, however.

The federal circuit and district courts began using this notice rule whenever federal labor statutes created the liability in issue. The courts have applied the notice rule in finding successor liability in employment discrimination cases—see, e.g., *Rojas v. TK Comm.* (5th Cir. 1996) (Title VII); *EEOC v. Vucitech* (7th Cir. 1988) (same)—and in cases on liability for pension obligations (delinquent pension contributions, termination liability and multi-employer withdrawal liability). E.g., *Chicago Truck Drivers, Helpers & Warehouse Workers Union Pension Fund v. Tasemkin* (7th Cir. 1995); *Stotter Div. of Graduate Plastic Co. v. District 65, United Auto Workers* (2d Cir. 1993). See also *Steinbach v. Hubbard* (9th Cir. 1994) (a claim for minimum wage under the Fair Labor Standards Act).

There is a split in the federal circuit courts, however, on whether there is a federal common law of successor liability under federal environmental statutes, such as CERCLA (the Superfund Act). Two Circuit Courts, the Sixth and the Ninth Circuits, say no, state law should apply. *Atchison, Topeka & Santa Fe Ry. Co. v. Brown & Bryant* (9th Cir. 1997); *Anspec Co. v. Johnson Controls, Inc.* (6th Cir. 1991). The Seventh Circuit has applied the *Golden State Bottling Co.* notice test. *North Shore Gas Co. v. Salomon* (7th Cir. 1998). See also *Smith Land & Improvement Corp. v. Celotex Corp.* (3d Cir. 1988). The smart money is on the application of state law, given the Supreme Court's clear hostility towards the development of a federal common law as expressed in the *Atherton* and *O'Melveny & Myers* cases in the mid-nineties. *O'Melveny & Myers v. FDIC* (U.S. 1994); *Atherton v. FDIC* (U.S. 1997).

The federal courts applying a federal law on successor liability in environmental cases are also split on whether they should stay with the traditional common law test for successor liability or if they should follow the more liberal substantial continuity rule. The substantial continuity rule relaxes the mere continuity plank of the common law test that requires that the ownership and business of the successor be identical to the ownership and business of the predecessor. E.g., *B.F. Goodrich v. Betkoski* (2d Cir. 1996).

§ 19. The Special Case of Collective Bargaining Agreements

The Supreme Court has decided a series of cases on the duty of a purchasing corporation to the employees of the selling corporation when those employees have a current collective bargaining agreement in place with the selling corporation. A collective bargaining agreement is fundamentally a contract between workers and an employer. Parties litigate claims arising out of a collective bargaining agreement under § 301 of the NLRA. Most collective bargaining agreements, but not all, have arbitration clauses creating duty to arbitrate on both sides.

Successors have been held bound by a duty to arbitrate under a predecessor's collective bargaining agreement if the agreement had not expired at the time of the acquisition and there is a substantial continuity of identity in the business enterprise before and after the acquisition. *John Wiley & Sons, Inc. v. Livingston* (U.S. 1964). In applying the standard the Court looks to whether the purchasing firm has continued the operations of the selling firm and has hired a significant percentage of the selling firm's employees. See *Howard Johnson Co. v. Detroit Local Joint Executive Bd.* (U.S. 1974).

The Supreme Court has also held the purchasing corporations to a lesser duty, the duty to bargain with the labor union of the selling corporation. Imposing a duty to bargain on a successor employer is not as severe as imposing a duty to arbitrate on a successor employer. *NLRB v. Burns Intern. Sec. Serv. Inc.* (U.S. 1972). A purchasing corporation under a duty to bargain is not bound to observe the substantive terms of the collective bargaining contract the union had negotiated with the selling corporation. The factual distinction between cases that requires a successor's duty to arbitrate as opposed to the lesser duty to bargain is less than clear in the case law.

Imposing a duty to bargain on a successor is significant for various reasons. It recognizes a bargaining relationship between an employer and a union and an agency relationship between a union and a group of employees. Without it, a union has to engage in an organizing drive, which is typically very costly and has an uncertain outcome. When the duty to bargain applies, the employer must bargain with the union over mandatory topics, risking an economic strike if a contract cannot be signed. Under the NLRA it is an unfair labor practice for an employer or a union to refuse to bargain collectively and the employer must meet at reasonable times and confer in good faith with respect to wages, hours, and other terms and conditions of employment. While the parties have an obligation to meet and confer in good faith, that obligation does not compel either party to agree to a proposal or require the making of a concession. Moreover, the new employer may be unable to institute changes unilaterally in mandatory topics without first bargaining to impasse. Finally, the duty to bargain forces the parties to disclose information in certain defined contexts. When, for example, an employer claims that it is financially unable to meet the union's demands, it must corroborate such claims on request.

The courts have made it clear that an asset purchaser cannot avoid a duty to bargain, or in an appropriate case a duty to arbitrate, by discriminating against employees of the seller because of their union status. For example, a new employer may not discover from the old employer the union sympathies of its employees and refuse to hire those identified as sympathetic. The cases suggest that, if a new employer maintains the old operations intact, hiring new, inexperienced, non-union employees in preference to experienced, union employees, judges will presume anti-union animus. By contrast, if operations substantially are changed so that experience in the old operation would be of little value in the new operation, no such inference is warranted.

§ 20. Liability Avoidance Scams and Counteracting Legal Rules

If only a portion of a firm's assets are being transferred, if a firm is being liquidated after a business failure, or if the seller values some significant assets or liabilities more highly than the buyer does, the parties typically will choose to structure the transaction as a sale of assets, rather than as a merger, and identify specifically which assets and liabilities are transferred. This is not always true in each case. For example, in a case in which the purchaser wants only some of the seller's assets, the parties could restructure the target before an acquisition, with a spin-off, for example, and use a statutory merger to acquire the desired assets after the restructuring. So long as the buyer pays fair market value for the assets it buys and applies the consideration received in the acquisition to the debts of the business, creditors of the seller are made better off by a rule that permits the parties to allocate assets and liabilities to the highest valuing user. If, on the other hand, the seller in the acquisition uses the transaction as a vehicle to avoid applying the money received to the debts of the business and instead distributes the consideration received to its shareholders, then creditors are worse off.

Opportunistic sellers have used three strategies to hurt the creditors. All three involve an asset sale. Following an asset sale those who control the seller, now a non-operating company holding passive assets (cash or stock in the purchaser) and still on the hook for all long-tail liabilities, attempt to distribute the assets to themselves and other shareholders ahead of the creditors.

First, they liquidate and dissolve the seller, passing the sale proceeds out in liquidation proceeds. The dissolution provisions of state corporate codes apply to control such distributions. Second, they cause the seller to declare either a one-time, extraordinary dividend or share redemption using the sale proceeds as the dividend or the repurchase payment. The *legal capital* statutes in state corporate codes and state statutes on *fraudulent conveyances* apply to the distributions.

And third (the mafia version), they cause the seller to enter into a variety of sweetheart deals with the controlling shareholders, milking the assets over time. Controlling shareholders can distribute corporate assets as excessive salary payments, through sales of the assets for less-than-fair-market value, through loans to shareholders at less-than-market interest rates, through guarantees of shareholder debt, through pledges to shareholders on loans from shareholders to the firm in which the firm defaults on the underlying debt and the assets are forfeited to the shareholders, and so on. Doctrines on breach of fiduciary duty, statutes on conflict-of-interest, and state statutes on fraudulent conveyances apply to this alternative.

In both the second and third alternatives, after the shareholders milk the seller of all its assets, the seller becomes a shell company, the shareholders stop the payment of the seller's annual state franchise fees, and the state dissolves the shell as a matter of law for non-payment.

The success of the three alternatives depends in part on the deficiencies in the countervailing law and in serendipity. If the claimants sit on their rights they lose them. *State bulk sales laws*, still in place in a dwindling number of states, force sellers in asset sales to notify all claimants of an asset sale to put them on notice of their potential vulnerability.

The doctrine of successor liability in asset sales that holds the purchaser liable for the debts of the seller is a doctrine that reflects our dissatisfaction with (and ignorance of, perhaps) these other legal protections.

A. Dissolution Procedures in State Corporate Codes

All state corporation codes provide for the dissolution of corporations. There is a majority, traditional approach and some modern innovations. Under the traditional approach, state codes have permitted corporations to dissolve and pay out any surplus to shareholders after paying off all known creditors. After dissolution, the corporation winds up its affairs, paying off its creditors and distributing any surplus to shareholders. Most traditional corporate law statutes bar claims of creditors who come forward after the statutorily mandated notice and claims period. As to known creditors, this system is satisfactory; if the asset seller receives fair value for the assets, existing creditors of the seller are no worse off and, when the seller dissolves, have an opportunity to present their claims for payment ahead of any distributions to shareholders.

But this statutory structure provides an opportunity for asset buyers and sellers to share the gains of jointly externalizing risk onto unknown future tort and environmental creditors—the *long-tail* or *contingent* claimants. The future victims cannot negotiate during the winding-up period with the dissolving firm to price the risk of future liabilities, and sellers will not internalize the full costs of their business decisions on potential tort victims or environmental claimants. Some limited protection is available under traditional statutes. E.g., MBCA § 105 (1979). This provision authorized suits against a dissolved corporation for two years after dissolution. Some state courts held that the provision barred claims that arose after the two-year period; other courts held the statute did not provide a statute of limitations but only affected a claimant's ability to sue a firm as opposed to its shareholders. If a long-tail claim matures shortly after the liquidation distributions to the selling firm shareholders, the claimants have only the statutory period, usually two or three years, to sue the shareholders individually and then only to the extent of their personal distribution (or a pro rata share of the claim if less). Long-tail claimants in this class can recover only by chasing a diffuse group of shareholders; other long-tail claimants are out of luck.

In recognition of the problems with the traditional provisions, the Model Business Corporation Act has gone through two major revisions, one in 1984 and another in 2000. The 1984 version, followed in several states, extends the claim period to five years from the traditional two- or three-year period on the assumption that most of the long-tail claims would arise during that period. MBCA § 14.07(c) (1984). At the same time the 1984 revision clarified that the section had the effect of a statute of limitations on long-term claims and not just a statement on the capacity of a dissolved firm to be sued. Under the Model Act, long-tail claims are barred unless made within five years of dissolution, unless based on a contingency or an event occurring *after* dissolution. MBCA § 14.07(d) (1984). When not barred, claims may be enforced against the dissolved corporation to the extent of undistributed assets and against shareholders to the extent of the shareholders' pro rata share of the obligation or the value of the assets distributed in liquidation, whichever is less. The 2000 MBCA amendments have taken a different tack, following the Delaware provisions noted below.

Delaware has recently taken an innovative approach. Like the traditional approach, the Delaware general corporate laws require that a dissolving corporation make provision to pay all contingent, conditional, or immature contractual claims known to the corporation—the traditional rule. DGCL §§ 280-282. Section 281(b) also requires, however, that a dissolving corporation formulate a plan of distribution to make such provision for claims "that have not been made known, or that have not arisen, but that, based on facts known to the corporation..., are likely to arise or to become known to the corporation...within ten years of the date of dissolution." If the amount provided is insufficient, claimants may pursue shareholders for amounts received in the liquidating distribution or their pro rata share of the claim, whichever is less, subject to the statute of limitations on the claim itself. DGCL § 282(a). But directors of a dissolved corporation are not liable personally if such a plan of distribution was formulated properly and the amounts set aside were reasonable at the time the plan was made. Id. § 281(c).

For shareholders in dissolving corporations who want to cut off long-tail claims, a safe harbor procedure is available. A dissolving corporation may petition the Court of Chancery to determine the amount and form of security that is

> reasonably likely to be sufficient to provide compensation for claims that have not been made known to the corporation or that have not risen but that, based on facts known to the corporation or successor entity, are likely to arise or to become known to the corporation or successor entity within 5 years after the date of dissolution or such longer period of time as the Court of Chancery may determine not to exceed 10 years after the date of dissolution.

DGCL § 280(c)(3). The court may appoint a guardian ad litem to represent the long-tail claimants. Id. On compliance with the court decree, shareholders are not liable for any claims begun after the three-year winding-up period established by § 278. DGCL § 282(b).

The MBCA 2000 amendments follow Delaware's lead. The amendments reduce the period of presenting claims after publication of notice from five years to three years and a new section, MBCA § 14.08, similar in effect to the Delaware provision, creates a court proceeding that gives directors and shareholders a safe harbor in providing for contingent claims that are not barred by publication. The dissolving firm provides security for claims that are reasonably estimated to arise after the effective date of dissolution.

B. Legal Capital or Insolvency Statutes

Limitations on dividends and redemptions are found in the statutes of all corporate codes. The statutes are in a state of evolution; a few states (including Delaware) have the old statutes (*legal capital statutes*) with par value shares, and most states have new provisions (*insolvency statutes*) that no longer depend on the par value concept. Section 6.40 of the Model Business Corporation Act, a modern statute, provides that no distribution may be made if, after giving it effect, (1) the corporation would not be able to pay its debts as they become due in the usual course of business (the *equity insolvency* test); or (2) the corporation's total assets would be less than the sum of its total liabilities plus the amount that would be needed, if the corporation were to be dissolved at the time of the distribution, to satisfy the preferential rights upon dissolution of shareholders whose preferential rights are superior to those receiving the distribution (the *balance sheet* test). Any director that votes for or assents to a distribution made in violation of § 6.40 is personally liable to the corporation for the amount of the illegal distribution. MBCA § 8.33. Any proceeding against a director must be brought within two years of the illegal distribution. Id. A director found liable can assert contribution rights against other directors and against shareholders who received part of an illegal distribution for the amount received if the shareholder knew the distribution was illegal when made. Id.

C. Fraudulent Conveyance Statutes

Fraudulent conveyance laws are aimed at protecting the creditors' right to execute judgments on assets of debtors in the event of defaults. If a debtor has transferred property to frustrate collection efforts by creditors, creditors may sue under state law to set aside any improper transfers and obtain a lien on the transferred property to the full extent of their claims. Trustees in bankruptcy (or debtors in possession) are empowered under federal law to recover for the benefit of creditors the value of any property improperly removed from the bankrupt debtor's estate. Fraudulent conveyance provisions are found in § 548 of the Federal Bankruptcy Code, 11 U.S.C.A. § 548, and in state acts, which are typically modeled on either the Uniform Fraudulent Conveyance Act (1918) (UFCA) or the newer Uniform Fraudulent Transfer Act (1984) (UFTA). A trustee in bankruptcy is also empowered to invoke state fraudulent conveyance law to invalidate pre-bankruptcy transfers. 11 U.S.C.A. § 544(b).

The UFTA and insolvency statutes such as § 6.40 of the Revised Model Business Corporation Act noted above overlap, but the UFTA is broader in scope. The Model Act applies only to distributions by a corporation to its shareholders "in respect of any of its shares." The UFTA § 5(a) applies to any transfer of property by any debtor to anybody and for any purpose whenever there is actual intent to defraud creditors or whenever the transferor receives value that is less than reasonably equivalent value. The difference between the value received and reasonably equivalent value is treated as a gratuitous transfer that creditors or their representative can recover under UFTA § 7. Moreover, UFTA § 8 does not recognize innocent receipt of a gratuitous fraudulent transfer as a defense.

The UFTA, like the UFCA before it, catches transfers that show an "actual intent to hinder, delay or defraud creditors" (the *actual intent* test). UFTA § 4(a)(1). More important, perhaps, is the *constructive intent* test in UFTA §§ 4(a)(2) & 5. A transfer is deemed fraudulent when the seller does not receive "reasonably equivalent value in exchange" and the seller's remaining assets are "unreasonably small in relation to the business" remaining (UFTA § 4(a)(2)(I)); the seller knew or should have known that it would "incur debts beyond [its] ability to pay as they became due" (UFTA § 4(a)(2)(ii)); or "the debtor was insolvent at that time or the debtor became insolvent as a result of the transfer" (UFTA § 5). Creditors whose claims attached before or after the transfer was made can use the first two theories of relief; creditors whose claims predate the transfer can also use the third theory.

Recently federal courts have struggled with whether the UFTA and its predecessor, the UFCA, provide relief for creditors in bankrupt companies that have recently undergone leveraged buy-outs (LBOs) or other leveraged recapitalizations. See, e.g., *Pay 'N Pak Stores v. Court Square Capital LTD* (9th Cir. 1998) (jury verdict against an application of a fraudulent conveyance act to a leveraged buy-out affirmed). See Chapter 1 for a description of an LBO. The fraudulent conveyance attack on failed LBOs has succeeded in a limited number of cases. In *Lippi v. City Bank* (9th Cir. 1992) and *United States v. Tabor Court Realty Corp.* (3d Cir. 1986), lenders to the purchasers in an LBO had their security interests set aside as fraudulent conveyances, and in *Lippi* and *Wieboldt Stores v. Schottenstein* (Ill. 1988), departing shareholders in the target had their stock sales set aside as fraudulent conveyances (they were constructive redemptions).

Most such claims fail, however. Plaintiffs often flounder under the heavy burden of proving that the target firm was insolvent at the time of the LBO. Parties to the LBO, the new equity owners and the new lenders (defendants in a fraudulent conveyance statute claim), do not invest unless they are convinced the firm can survive. Their return on their investment depends on the success of the releveraged firm. Moreover, the departing directors, to protect themselves from claims based on breach of fiduciary duty, often hire expert consultants that provide *solvency opinions*, opinions that the firm, immediately after the LBO, will be solvent. On the other hand, courts often find that management skills and access to new credit are not enough as a matter of law to constitute reasonably equivalent consideration. E.g., *Moody v. Security Pacific Business Credit, Inc.* (3d Cir. 1992) (new management skills and new access to credit not reasonably equivalent value as a matter of law, but firm solvent at time of LBO); cf. *SPC Plastics Corp. v. Griffith* (6th Cir. 1998) (summary judgment for debtor affirmed on grounds that new management skills and new access to credit could not be equivalent value; summary judgment for debtor on insolvency reversed).

D. State Bulk Transfer or Bulk Sales Acts (Article 6 of the Uniform Commercial Code)

States enacted bulk sale legislation in the early 1900s to remedy a type of fraud on creditors perpetuated by unscrupulous trading merchants. A merchant would acquire his stock in trade on credit, then sell his entire inventory (in bulk) to a single purchaser and abscond with the proceeds, leaving creditors unpaid. The creditors had a right to sue the merchant on the unpaid debts, but that right often was of little practical value. Even if the merchant-debtor was found and served success-fully with process, those creditors who succeeded in obtaining a judgment often were unable to satisfy it because the defrauding seller had spent or hidden the sale proceeds. Nor did the creditors ordinarily have recourse to the merchandise sold. The transfer of the inventory to an innocent buyer, a good faith purchaser, effectively immunized the goods from the reach of the seller's creditors.

The states believed that the law of fraudulent conveyances, on the books at that time, although helpful in some situations, was too narrow. When the buyer in bulk was in league with the seller or paid less than full value for the inventory, fraudulent conveyance law enabled the defrauded creditors to avoid the sale and apply the trans-ferred inventory toward the satisfaction of their claims against the seller. But fraudulent convey-ance law provided no remedy when purchasers

bought for adequate value and in good faith—
without reason to know of the seller's intention to
pocket the proceeds and disappear. State legislatures responded with *bulk sales* laws. The Uniform
Commissioners on State Laws simplified and codi-
fied the state laws in a *Bulk Transfer Act* added as
Article 6 of the Uniform Commercial Code in the
early fifties. All 50 states adopted a version of the
article. By 1987 the Commissioners had a radical
change of heart and recommended that states
repeal entirely the Bulk Transfer Act or replace it
with a much tamer *Bulk Sales Act*. As of early
1998, 35 states (including Florida) had repealed
their Bulk Transfer Act outright and eight states
(including California) had adopted the Revised
Article 6 Bulk Sales Act. New York still retains a
version of the Bulk Transfer Act.

Common to all bulk sales laws is the
imposition of a duty on the buyer whenever it purchases the stock in trade of a seller, a sale *in bulk*,
to notify the seller's creditors of the impending
sale. The laws applied only when the seller traded
an inventory (stock) and when the purchaser did
not agree to assume the seller's debts in full on the
acquisition of the stock. If the purchaser does
assume the seller's debts, the purchaser must be
solvent after the assumption and must give
written notice of the assumption within 30 days of
the sale. UCC § 6-103(3)(j) (1987 Text).

Original Article 6—the Bulk Transfer Act—
requires that a purchaser send notice 10 days

before whichever occurs first: the purchaser closes, the purchaser takes possession of the goods, or the purchaser pays for the goods. In those jurisdictions that have adopted optional § 6-106 in their Bulk Transfer Act, the purchaser also must assure that the new consideration for the transfer is applied to pay debts of the transferor.

The buyer's failure to comply with these and any other statutory duties generally affords the seller's creditors a remedy analogous to the remedy for fraudulent conveyances: The creditors acquire the right to set aside the sale and can reach the transferred inventory in the hands of the buyer. Like its predecessors, the Bulk Transfer Act is remarkable in that it obligates buyers in bulk to incur costs to protect the interests of the seller's creditors, with whom they usually have no relationship. Even more striking is that the Bulk Transfer Act affords creditors a remedy against a good faith purchaser for full value without notice of any wrongdoing on the part of the seller.

Compliance with the provisions of the Bulk Transfer Act can be burdensome, particularly when the transferor has a large number of creditors. When the transferor is actively engaged in business at a number of locations, assembling a current list of creditors may not be possible. Mailing a notice to each creditor may prove costly. When the goods that are the subject of the transfer are located in several jurisdictions, the transferor may be obligated to comply with Article 6 as enacted in each jurisdiction. The widespread enactment of differing amendments makes compliance with Article 6 in multiple-state transactions problematic. Moreover, the Bulk Transfer Act requires compliance even when there is no reason to believe that the transferor is conducting a fraudulent transfer, e.g., when the transferor is scaling down the business but remaining available to creditors.

Many now believe that the benefits that compliance with the Bulk Transfer Act affords to creditors are insubstantial and do not justify the burdens and risks that the article imposes upon good faith purchasers of business assets. The Bulk Transfer Act requires that notice be sent only 10 days before the transferee takes possession of the goods or pays for them, whichever happens first. Given the delay between sending the notice and its receipt, creditors have scant opportunity to avail themselves of a judicial or nonjudicial remedy before the transfer has been consummated. In some cases the Bulk Transfer Act has the unintended effect of injuring, rather than aiding, creditors of the seller by discouraging the sales of a business. Those purchasers who recognize the burdens and risks that Article 6 imposes upon them sometimes agree to purchase only at a reduced price. Others refuse to purchase at all, leaving the creditors to realize only the liquidation value, rather than the going concern value, of the business goods.

The 1987 Bulk Sales Act reduces significantly the burdens and risks imposed upon good-faith buyers of business assets while increasing the protection afforded to creditors. There are numerous changes, among the most important: The new article applies only when the buyer has notice, or after reasonable inquiry would have notice, that the seller will not continue to operate the same or a similar kind of business after the sale. UCC § 6-102(1)(c). When the seller is indebted to a large number of persons (over 200), the buyer need neither obtain a list of those persons nor send individual notices to each person but instead may give notice by filing with a state official. UCC §§ 6-105(2) & 6-104(2). The notice period has also increased from 10 days to 45 days. UCC § 6-105(5). A buyer who makes a good faith effort to comply with the requirements of this article or to exclude the sale from the application of this article, or who acts on the good faith belief that this article does not apply to the sale, is not liable for noncompliance. UCC § 6-107(3). A buyer's noncompliance does not render the sale ineffective or otherwise affect the buyer's title to the goods; rather, the liability of a noncomplying buyer is for damages caused by the noncompliance. UCC §§ 6-107(1) & 6-107(8). Finally, the bulk sales law of the jurisdiction of the seller's chief executive office or place of business controls. UCC § 6-103(1) & (2).

To avoid the time, effort and potential disruption of complying with bulk sales acts, parties to asset acquisitions may agree to waive compliance based upon the seller's agreement to indemnify the purchaser against seller creditor claims. If the purchaser does not trust the indemnification protection and there is otherwise insufficient security (no escrow), then wise purchasers comply with the act.

§ 21. Purchasing Assets in Bankruptcy

When a target firm is in bankruptcy, a purchaser is usually limited to an asset acquisition. The purchase of the stock of an insolvent firm makes little economic sense; the stock is worthless. Moreover, a merger of an insolvent firm into a solvent firm attaches the liabilities of the insolvent firm to the solvent firm's assets to the glee of the insolvent firm's creditors and to the pain of the solvent firm's owners. A purchaser seeks the assets of the target in bankruptcy free of its excessive liabilities.

The federal bankruptcy code permits insolvent firms to sell their assets in whole as well as in parcels to maximize the size of the pool of funds available to unpaid creditors. Bankruptcy Code § 1123 (all subsequent reference to sections in this subchapter are to the Bankruptcy Code). During an ongoing bankruptcy proceeding, a buyer can purchase assets from a secured lender who has foreclosed, from a bankruptcy trustee (a §363(f) sale), or pursuant to a plan of reorganization in a Chapter 11 proceeding.

As a general rule, Chapter 11 cleanses a debtor of its pre-Chapter 11 obligations (except as they are included in the capital restructuring of the firm pursuant to a plan of reorganization). A buyer from a debtor in Chapter 11 (whether pursuant to § 363 or a plan of reorganization) may nevertheless face some risk that it may succeed to certain pre-existing liabilities of the troubled seller, even where the sale purports to be free and clear of claims. In particular, there is an issue over whether a court can discharge future product liability or environmental claims in a Chapter 11 proceeding. To the extent these future claims are not dischargeable, a sale order (under § 363(f)) or order confirming a plan (discharging claims under § 1141) may be ineffective to cleanse the assets being sold. Thus, a buyer of substantially all the assets of the bankrupt party may be subject to the risk of liability for these claims under state law successor liability doctrines.

If an asset purchaser has taken title to a contaminated site, CERCLA liability follows the asset, even if the contamination occurred prior to the bankruptcy proceeding. See *In re Chateaugay Corp.* (2d Cir. 1991) (EPA cleanup orders survive bankruptcy). Such an asset purchaser is liable under CERCLA as a current owner for all contamination at the site regardless of when it occurred (unless she can use the very narrow *innocent purchaser* defense). CERCLA is silent on two related questions—the successor's liability when the environmental claim arises out of the disposal of hazardous substances off-site by a predecessor prior to its bankruptcy proceeding and the successor's liability when the claim arises out of the operation by a predecessor of a contaminated site owned by another party. Sometimes the claims are linked in one fact pattern. A purchaser in an asset acquisition may not know about the off-site disposal (it was performed by an operating unit of the seller that either no longer existed or was not acquired by the asset purchaser, for example) nor about the predecessor's operation of a contaminated site.

The federal courts have not settled the question of whether a purchaser in an asset acquisition may avoid such liabilities with a disclaimer in the acquisition agreement. Because § 363(f) on purchases from a trustee states that a sale is free and clear only of "interests" in property, some courts have suggested that assets cannot be sold free and clear of all claims. E.g., *The Ninth Avenue Remedial Group v. Allis-Chalmers Corp.* (N.D. Ind. 1996) (no, if claim arises after the bankruptcy proceeding has been concluded). These decisions appear to be inconsistent with the approach of the vast majority of bankruptcy courts, as well as with sound bankruptcy policy. As a consequence, cautious buyers in asset acquisitions under § 363 request some or all of the following: (a) adequate notice to potential claimants of the hearing at which the court will be asked to approve the sale free and clear of all claims; (b) a specific finding by the bankruptcy court that the sale is free and clear of claims; and (c) a decree in the order approving the sale enjoining claimants from pursuing the buyer or the purchased assets.

In contrast to § 363(f), § 1141(c) of the Bankruptcy Code dealing with Chapter 11 plans of reorganization specifically refers to claims. It states that any property "dealt with" by a plan is "free and clear of all claims and interests of creditors, equity security holders, and of general partners in the debtor." Thus, the interpretive issue arising under § 363(f) creating uncertainty over the ability to sell free and clear of claims should not arise with respect to sales under a plan.

CHAPTER 6

FEDERAL LAW ON ACQUISITIONS OF OR BY PUBLICLY-TRADED CORPORATIONS

Federal securities law supplements state corporate codes and, for acquisitions involving publicly-traded companies, imposes additional procedural requirements. Some of the requirements impact the basic acquisition procedure or process. Other requirements from the same acts penalize acquisition participants for fraudulent or misleading disclosures whether mandated or voluntary.

§ 22. Proxy Regulations and Shareholder Voting on Acquisitions in Publicly-Traded Corporations

When stockholders vote on acquisitions, state law requires generally that they receive adequate information from their managers on the details of the transaction. State corporate codes often do not detail the specific kinds of information that stockholders should have when they vote. See, e.g., DGCL § 251(c). The section only requires that the directors send the shareholders a notice containing a copy of the agreement or a "brief summary...as the directors shall deem advisable." A 1998 amendment to § 251(b), however, requires the directors' resolution approving the merger (which, along with the full agreement, is of record at the shareholder meeting on the merger) to "declar[e] its advisability." Some state court case law has developed, under the rubric of a common law on fiduciary duty, on the obligation of a firm to notify its shareholders of all material facts in a transaction, particularly if the transaction creates a conflict of interest for senior managers. Management buyouts (LBOs) and parent-subsidiary mergers that cash out minority shareholders are the classic examples. Otherwise state law on the matter is basically open-ended.

Federal securities law stands in stark contrast to state law. If a firm is publicly held, then § 14(a) of the Securities and Exchange Act of 1934 and the rules promulgated thereunder apply to the company's *proxy solicitations*. A company is publicly held if it must register one or more classes of its securities under § 12 of the 1934 Act. A company must register any security traded on a national stock exchange or any security held by over 500 shareholders when the firm has $10 million in assets. Exchange Act § 12(a) & (g), Rule 12g-1.

A proxy is a delegation of voting power by a shareholder to an agent, the *proxy holder*; it is a creation of state law. The SEC rules regulate the solicitation of proxies, requiring that a *proxy statement* accompany all solicitations and controlling the content and form of the proxy document itself, the *proxy card*.

Since most large firms must solicit proxies from their shareholders in order to do business at shareholder meetings, the rules have substantial bite. Ordinary business, such as the election of directors, requires an affirmative vote of those attending the meeting and a minimum attendance, entitled a *quorum*. The diffusion of shareholder holding in most publicly-traded firms requires that the firm solicit proxies to have a quorum. In acquisitions, since the required vote is usually a majority of the outstanding shares, a proxy solicitation is necessary to gather enough affirmative votes to pass on the board recommendation. Moreover, even if a registered firm does not solicit proxies for a shareholder meeting, the Exchange Act requires a firm to mail an "information statement" that is substantially the same as a proxy statement. Exchange Act § 14(c), Reg. 14C.

While most of the popular focus on proxy regulations pays attention to shareholder voting for seats on a corporation's board of directors, the rules apply to all matters subject to a shareholder vote. Thus the regulations promulgated by the SEC specifically cover proxy solicitations for votes required by state corporate codes for mergers, asset acquisitions, and reorganizations. The regulations are very detailed on the information that acquisition parties must disclose and yet contain open-ended admonitions to add all other material facts as well. The detail in the schedules can be important even for closely-held firms not specifically covered by the Exchange Act. They provide a safe harbor of sorts for protection from second-guessing by state judges under the open-ended requirements of state corporate law. The rules give guidance to firm officials on what will satisfy the state codes.

A. The Timing Requirements of Regulation 14A

Regulation 14A, passed by the SEC under the authority of § 14(a) of the Exchange Act, consists of 13 rules. Under Rule 14a-3(a), when an acquisition is the subject of a shareholder vote, no solicitation subject to the rules may be made "unless each person solicited is concurrently furnished or has previously been furnished with a written proxy statement containing information specified in Schedule 14A."

The SEC has recently liberalized the definition of "solicitation." Old Rule 14a-12 severely restricted communications between a firm and its shareholders until shareholders had been mailed a formal multi-page proxy statement. New Rule 14a-12 permits both oral and written communications before the filing of a proxy statement (whether or not the solicitation involves a business combination transaction). The communications must be filed on the date of first use, no form proxy may be furnished, and a legend must be included advising shareholders to read the proxy statement and indicating where to find participant information.

The SEC also has eliminated the condition in old Rule 14a-12 that a written proxy statement meeting the requirements of Regulation 14A be sent or given to security holders, once solicited, at the earliest practicable date. As revised, Rule 14a-12 requires that a definitive proxy statement be furnished to security holders only when a form of proxy is either given to or requested from security holders.

Preliminary copies of the proxy statement and the form of the proxy must be filed with the commission at least 10 days before the final material is used. Rule 14a-6(a). In addition, copies of all literature in *definitive* form must be mailed, concurrently with its distribution, to the commission and to each exchange on which any security of the issuer is listed. Rule 14a-6(c). The soliciting firm may mail the preliminary proxy statement to shareholders but usually waits until the proxy statement is final or definitive because the firm can send the proxy card only with the definitive statement. Issuers may file preliminary proxy material confidentially with the SEC. Rule 14a-(6)(2).

If the SEC staff decides to review the preliminary proxy material, the offeror must await staff comments before mailing the definitive materials. Only when the SEC staff and the firm have negotiated about the SEC concerns can the definitive materials be mailed to shareholders.

Under newly-revised Rule 14a-6(e), preliminary proxy material about a business combination will be confidential only if none of the parties makes any public communication relating to the transaction that goes beyond the very limited information permitted under Rule 135. The transaction also cannot be a "roll-up" or a Rule 13e-3 going-private transaction. Since Rule 135 is very narrow, it allows disclosure of only the name of the parties involved in the exchange, the securities to be exchanged, the anticipated timing, manner, and purpose of the offering, and the basis upon which the exchange may be made. In most cases parties will make public announcements that contain more information than is specified in Rule 135, and their preliminary filing materials will then be available through the SEC's electronic website.

There is no federally-mandated time period between the date the offeror mails the proxy material and the date of the security holder meeting, but an exception dominates practice. If proxy statements incorporate by reference other public filings of the firm (which often is the case), then the statement must be delivered 20 days before the date of the shareholder vote. Note D.3 to SEC Schedule 14A. In any event, state law provides the universal minimum notice for shareholder meetings. In Delaware, for example, a corporation must mail notice to its shareholders before any meeting, annual or special, not less than 10 days and not more than 60 days before the date of the meeting. DGCL § 222(b). The proxy solicitation usually accompanies any notice of the meeting required by state corporate codes.

In sum, publicly-traded firms usually solicit proxies by mail 10 to 60 days in advance of a shareholder meeting on an acquisition ratification. Firms intent on filing definitive proxy materials with their required state notices must have filed with the SEC their preliminary proxy materials over 10 days in advance of the proxy solicitation mailing to account for potential delays resulting from SEC comments.

B. The Proxy Form and the Disclosure Requirements of Schedule 14A Pertaining to Shareholder Votes on Acquisitions

The proxy form must itself indicate in boldface type whether or not the proxy is solicited on behalf of the firm's board. Rule 14a-6(h). The proxies can confer authority to vote at only one meeting. Rule 14a-4(d)(2). The proxy must identify *clearly and impartially* any acquisition or reorganization question submitted to a vote and permit the security holder to choose "between approval or disapproval...or abstention." Rule 14a-4(a)(3) & (b)(1). General discretionary proxies, proxies in which a shareholder delegates general voting authority to the proxy holder, are prohibited.

The first five items of Schedule 14A (the numbered items detail what must be included in a proxy information statement) apply to all proxy statements, regardless of the type of action proposed. They call for, among other things, information with respect to the revocability of any executed proxy, dissenters' appraisal rights, the identity of those soliciting the proxy, the special interest of the solicitors and others connected with the solicitors, and a description of the issuer's outstanding securities and their principal holders.

Item 14 applies specifically to votes on acquisitions. Item 14 applies if any action is to be taken with respect to any transaction involving (1) the merger or consolidation of the registrant into or with any other person or of any other person into or with the registrant, (2) the acquisition by the registrant or any of its security holders of securities of another person, (3) the acquisition by the registrant of any other going business or of the assets thereof, (4) the sale or other transfer of all or any substantial part of the assets of the registrant, or (5) the liquidation or dissolution of the registrant. Subsection (a) in Item 14 calls for information about the transaction in issue, and subsection (b) calls for information about both parties to the transaction. New SEC rules limit the need to provide financial information about both the target and the acquirer in cash mergers and the need to provide financial information about the target in stock swap mergers if the securities received are exempt from Securities Act registration.

Two items apply to recapitalizations. Item 12 applies to single-firm exchange reorganizations—

"if action is to be taken with respect to the modification of any class of securities of the registrant, or the issuance or authorization for issuance of securities of the registrant in exchange for outstanding securities...." Item 11 applies to shareholder votes on the authorization or issuance of additional securities "otherwise than for exchange for outstanding securities of the registrant." It would include votes on amendments to certificates of incorporation that authorize the issuance of additional securities, for example.

For our purposes, Item 14 is the most significant. Item 14(b)(2) applies to firms that meet the requirements of Form S-2 or S-3 (companies that have been subject to the periodic reporting obligations of the federal securities acts for three years or one year respectively). Subsection (b)(3) applies to all other firms and is thus the base requirement. Subsections (b)(2) and (b)(3) also incorporate by reference parts of two other SEC regulations, Regulation S-X and Regulation S-K. Regulation S-X specifies the accounting conventions that filing parties must use in their required financial documents—balance sheets, income statements, and cash flow statements. Regulation S-K is more general and contains a variety of requirements. There is a heavy emphasis in the regulation on disclosures about past history and performance; there are only a few, narrow requirements for projections and predictions. See, e.g., Reg. S-K, Item 102(4) & (5) (estimates on reserves); Item 201(c) (future dividends); and Item

303(a) (estimates of liquidity, capital resources and unusual events).

The primary effect of the SEC proxy rules and schedules is to expose a firm soliciting proxies to potential litigation from either the SEC or its shareholders in the event that (1) the firm does not comply with the details of Schedule 14A, (2) the firm affirmatively misrepresents a material fact in its Schedule 14A, or (3) the firm omits a fact necessary to make a written statement not materially misleading. It is the SEC's view that information specifically required by Schedule 14A must be disclosed regardless of materiality. Any negligent omissions by the soliciting firm subject them to liability under Rule 14a-9, the anti-fraud rule. See, e.g., *Gerstle v. Gamble-Skogmo, Inc.* (2d Cir. 1973). When an affirmatively misleading statement or omitted information *is* material, the fact that it is not specifically called for by Schedule 14A does not foreclose the possibility of a violation of Rule 14a-9.

§ 23. Tender Offer Regulations on Stock Acquisitions of Publicly-Traded Corporations: The Williams Act

A. Third-Party Tender Offers

The 1968 Williams Act, which added several sections, most notably §§ 13(d) and (e), and 14(d) and (e) to the Securities and Exchange Act of 1934, regulates tender offers—public announcements that a bidder will buy stock in a publicly-traded company if tendered to a deposit agent at a set price (or in exchange for a set value of an offeror's securities), usually in excess of the current market price (the *tender offer premium*). Bidders generally condition their offers on receipt of a minimum number of shares and may limit the number they are willing to accept. The Williams Act and its accompanying SEC regulations impose various structural requirements on an offer's form and also require bidders to make comprehensive and detailed disclosures when their offers commence (a Schedule TO). The SEC now requires a plain English summary sheet as well. In addition, the Act prohibits bidders from engaging in open-market purchases while an offer is alive.

The requirements on a tender offer's form prescribe: a 20-day minimum offering period (SEC Rule 14e-1), though most tender offers are open longer; shareholder withdrawal rights coextensive with the offering period (Rule 14d-7(a)); withdrawal rights after 60 days from the initial offer if the offeror has failed to close on the tenders (SEA § 14(d)(5)); pro rata acceptance for over-subscribed offers (Rule 14d-8); nondiscrimination among target shareholders (Rule 14d-10(a)(1)); and the extension of any price increase during the tender offer to all shareholders who have already tendered (Rule 14d-10(a)(2)). Also, during the tender offer, purchases by the bidder "otherwise than pursuant to such tender offer" (Rule 14e-5) and any short tenders by offerees (Rule 10b-4(b)) are prohibited by SEC rules as "manipulative or deceptive device[s] or contrivance[s]" and "fraudulent, deceptive or manipulative acts or practices" under § 14(e) of the Securities Exchange Act of 1934. Rule 14d-11 permits bidders in tender offers to provide for a period of between 3 and 20 business days after the expiration of a tender offer during which shares could be tendered without withdrawal rights.

All the requirements specified in § 14(d) of the 1934 Act and the 14d series of rules promulgated thereunder (Regulation 14D) apply only to tender offers for a class of voting equity securities registered under § 12 of the 1934 Act, that is, for voting equity securities of publicly-traded corporations. The requirements in § 14(e) and the rules promulgated thereunder apply whether or not the offer is subject to Regulation 14D. Section 14(e) is a general anti-fraud rule and authorizes the SEC to pass rules against fraudulent practices in all tender offers. Note, for example, that the minimum 20-day offering period in Rule 14e-1 thus applies to all tender offers (including tender offers for debt securities), not just tender offers for the voting stock of publicly-traded companies.

The Tender Offer Dance. The bidder typically posts a summary announcement of a tender offer in the *Wall Street Journal* and makes a Rule 14d-5 demand on the target. The target must, within three days, mail the bidder's tender offer materials to its shareholders or provide a shareholder list so the bidder can do a mailing. The bidder files its Schedule TO with the SEC, delivers a copy of the schedule to the target and to all national exchanges on which the target's stock is traded, and on the same day mails to the shareholders of the target firm portions of the Schedule, an *Offer to Purchase* and a *Letter of Transmittal*. The Offer, usually over 30 pages, sets forth the terms of the offer—the number of shares to be purchased, the offer price and the length of time the offer will be open—and additional information—details on withdrawal rights, discussion of tax consideration and the conditions of the offer.

Under SEC Rules, a tender offer commences when the bidder first publishes or gives security holders the means to tender securities in the offer (sends a letter of transmittal). To deter dissemination of false offers, the SEC adopted Rule 14e-8 prohibiting bidders from announcing an offer without an intent to commence the offer within a reasonable time, with an intent to manipulate stock prices, or without a reasonable belief that the bidder will have the means to purchase the securities sought. Public announcements of a tender offer trigger an obligation to file with the SEC all written communications upon their first use.

The SEC staff reviews the filed Schedule TO and may return comments to the bidder. The bidder and the SEC negotiate the comments while the tender offer is open. If unsatisfied by the bidder's responses, the SEC may ask the bidder to send additional information to the target shareholders and may ask the bidder to extend the tender offer period so that shareholders can consider the new material.

Shareholders respond by tendering their shares through a named intermediary, usually a commercial bank, named the *paying agent*. They attach the Letter of Transmittal to their shares; the paying agent accumulates the shares and pays all shareholders when the offer expires and the bidder accepts the tenders. If a shareholder wishes to withdraw shares, she must submit a *letter of withdrawal* accompanied by a *signature guarantee,* verifying that the signature of the shareholder is authentic. Shareholders often wait until the last minute before tendering their shares in the hope that better offers will materialize. As the expiration date approaches, brokers, acting on behalf of shareholders, may submit a *notice of guaranteed delivery*, guaranteeing that the broker will deliver shares within five business days; the paying agent will include the shares guaranteed in the offer.

The target firm, within 10 days of the commencement of the tender offer, must send a notice to its shareholders recommending, rejecting, expressing no opinion and remaining neutral, or stating that it is unable to take a position (Rule 14e-2). If the tender offer has been negotiated ahead of time (the normal case), the target will issue its affirmative recommendation in the form of a Schedule 14D-9. Whenever the target recommends that its security holders accept or reject the offer to tender, the firm must file with the SEC and deliver a

Schedule 14D-9 to its shareholders, the bidder and any national stock exchanges on which the stock is traded. The target's obligation to file a full Schedule 14D-9 arises on the day the target first makes a solicitation or recommendation with respect to a commenced (and not merely announced) tender offer or within 10 days of the offer, whichever is first. If the target begins to buy its own stock in response to the third-party tender offer, it must file a Rule 13e-1 Statement and if the issuer stock repurchase is in the form of a competing tender offer, the issuer also files and disseminates its own Schedule TO.

B. Issuer Tender Offers

An offer by a corporation to purchase its own outstanding securities is a form of recapitalization known as an *issuer tender offer*. An offer by someone other than the issuer is a *third-party tender offer*. Thus far in our discussion of § 14(d) of the 1934 Act and the SEC rules thereunder, we have been assuming a third-party tender offer. Issuer tender offers for the equity securities of a reporting company must comply with Rule 13e-4. All issuer tender offers, like all third-party tender offers, must comply with §14(e) of the 1934 Act. Rule 13e-4 imposes on issuer tender offers disclosure, form and timing requirements identical to those imposed on third-party tender offers noted above. Firms registering issuer tender offers also file a Schedule TO.

C. Going-Private Transactions

The SEC has also passed a series of rules and a schedule under a general grant of authority under § 13(e) of the 1934 Exchange Act, an open-ended antifraud provision on issuer stock repurchases, aimed at regulating *going-private transactions* (Rules 13e-3 to 13e-100 (Schedule 13E-3)). In a going-private transaction, a publicly-traded company—that is, a company that reports under § 12 of the 1934 Act—buys back enough of its shares to transform itself into a company whose stock is no longer registered. A publicly-traded company becomes a privately-held company. The consideration offered in the transaction to selling shareholders is usually cash or debt securities in the issuer, or a combination of the two. The stock repurchase can come in many forms: an issuer cash tender offer, a cash merger or a cash-for-assets acquisition.

There are major differences between Schedule 13E-3 for going-private issuer repurchases and Schedule TOs for issuer and third-party tender offers. Item 8 of Schedule 13E-3 incorporates by reference Item 1014 of Regulation M-A, which requires a statement on the fairness of a going-private transaction with supporting rationale. By requiring a statement on fairness, the issuer becomes liable on the assertion under the general antifraud provisions of the securities acts if the statement is misleading. All material factors behind the statement must be itemized and disclosed. In particular, Item 1015 in Regulation M-A requires the disclosure of all reports or appraisals from outside parties materially relating to the fairness of the offer. Schedule 13E-3, Item 9. In a Schedule 13E-3, the issuer, as a fiduciary to the selling shareholders, must, in essence, disclose all its valuation information, while outside bidders can presumably be more secretive.

Rule 13e-3 provides an exemption from a Schedule 13E-3 filing for second-step cleanup transactions occurring within one year after a tender offer by a non-affiliate, if the second-step consideration offered is at least equal to the highest consideration offered in the tender offer. See Rule 13e-3(g)(1). The rule has significant application problems, however.

§ 24. Using Securities as Consideration: The Prospectus Filing Requirements Under the Securities Act of 1933

The Securities Act of 1933 protects the purchasers of securities, broadly defined to include both debt and equity investment securities, in *public offerings*. In the classic public offering a firm sells securities to the public as a means of raising capital to fund its business. If a firm offers securities to the public, defined roughly as over 35 or so people, the firm must register the sale under the Securities Act of 1933. The 1933 Act applies to all major firm acquisitions in which the target shareholders receive investment securities (stock or debt) in the bidder, rather than cash, and the number of target shareholders is large. The SEC construes the purchasing firm's distribution of securities to the selling firm shareholders to be a public offering if the number of selling firm shareholders is large. SEC Rule 145.

A. Effect of the 1933 Act on Exchange Tender Offers

If an acquisition takes the form of an exchange tender offer—that is, a bidder makes a public offer to exchange target stock for stock or debt in the buyer (or the buyer's parent)—the offer is regulated under the Williams Act sections and the SEC rules promulgated thereunder as noted above. Yet the SEC also construes the offer to be a public offering of securities by the buyer to the holders of stock in the target. This brings into play the rules and regulations of the Securities Act of 1933, adding a layer of 1933 Act filings to the Williams Act filings. A third level of filings is required if the exchange tender offer stipulates that the right to vote the stock passes on tender. Such a tender offer may become a proxy solicitation and come under proxy solicitation requirements. Unless the buyer can qualify under one of the narrow exemptions to the 1933 Act (such as the private offering exemption)—an unlikely event—the Act affects the form and timing of exchange tender offers.

The supplemental filings add considerable expense and timing hurdles to the Williams Act regulations that a cash tender offer does not have to satisfy. Moreover, the buyer's stock held by the target shareholders after the exchange is subject to resale restrictions. Many assume that the target shareholders who have exchanged target shares for buyer securities in an exchange tender offer may immediately turn those securities into cash by selling them in the markets. This assumption is false. The SEC has developed a *presumptive underwriter* doctrine in a series of no-action letters that applies to target shareholders who receive a substantial amount (around 10 percent) of the block of buyer's stock used in the acquisition. If the doctrine applies, the shareholder must either file a full registration statement for the resale or qualify under Rule 145(d) or Rule 144, discussed in the next section. See SEC No-Action Letters on E.H. Crump Companies, Inc. (avail. Oct. 18, 1979), MCI Communications (avail. Jan. 11, 1975), Barnett Banks of Fla., Inc. (avail. Dec. 13, 1976). Outside the safe harbor rules, the contours of the doctrine are hazy.

The following paragraphs are a brief summary of the requirements of the 1933 Act on exchange tender offers.

The SEC permits purchasing firms to commence their tender offers on the filing of and prior to the effective date of a registration statement. To commence an exchange offer early (before effectiveness of a registration statement), a bidder must file a registration statement relating to the securities offered and include in the preliminary prospectus all information, including pricing information, necessary for investors to make an informed investment decision. Bidders also must disseminate the prospectus and related letter of transmittal to all security holders and file a tender offer statement with the SEC before the exchange offer can commence. Early commencement is at the option of the bidder. Exchange offers can commence as early as the filing of a registration statement, or on a later date selected by the bidder up to the date of effectiveness. If a bidder does not commence its exchange offer before effectiveness of the related registration statement, then the exchange offer would need to commence on or shortly after the date of effectiveness.

The registration statement must contain specified information about the security, the issuer and the underwriters (investment bankers who place the security). In filing a registration statement, a buyer may choose to use either Form S-1 or a special form for acquisitions, Form S-4. If using Form S-4, the buyer must include, among other items, information about the terms of the transaction (including pro forma financials for the projected combined firm), information about itself and information about the target. An acquirer does not need to provide financial statements for a non-reporting (not publicly-traded) target when the acquirer's security holders are not voting on the transaction and the non-reporting target is less than 20 percent the size of the acquirer. Otherwise, the non-reporting target company disclosure requirement is limited to one year of financial statements. The parties can use a Form S-4 filing to satisfy both the buyer's Schedule TO and the target's Schedule 14D-9 filing requirements if the parties are careful to integrate any added informational requirements in the Schedules into the S-4.

Once a firm files a registration statement with the SEC, the agency reviews the materials and, if satisfied, declares the registration statement to be "effective." A registration statement, according to the 1933 Act, automatically becomes effective 20 days after filing unless the Commission declares it effective sooner or takes action to toll the running of the period. In practice the SEC demands that all registrants waive the 20-day period. See SEC Rule 473 (providing for a paragraph on the cover of a registration statement that effects a continuing amendment) and SEC Rule 461 (used by the SEC to condition acceleration on the issuer's filing a delaying amendment). The delaying amendment gives the SEC time to screen the registration statements and decide which ones to review thoroughly. Security holders may tender their securities prior to effectiveness of the registration statement but the bidder cannot accept the tenders until the SEC declares the registration statement to be effective. SEC Rule 162. Once a bidder has sent target shareholders a preliminary prospectus and supplements containing material changes, if any, it need not deliver a final prospectus. In adopting the rules the SEC staff noted the potential for disadvantage to a bidder in an exchange tender offer if the staff review process causes a delay in declaring the registration statement effective. The release stated that the SEC staff is committed to the expeditious review of exchange offers so that such offers could compete more effectively with cash tender offers.

Regulation M prohibits the bidder or target from purchasing bidder securities after the exchange offer is commenced (SEC Reg. M, 17 C.F.R. 242.100 to 242.105, complementing Rule 14e-5, noted above, which prohibits purchases of target securities once the offer is announced).

B. Effect of the 1933 Act on Stock Swap Statutory Mergers and Stock-for-Asset Acquisitions

If the purchasing firm uses its own stock in the stock swap merger or a stock-for-assets acquisition and the target is a publicly-traded corporation, the SEC adds the disclosure requirements of the 1933 Act to the proxy solicitation rules of the 1934 Exchange Act (see § 22) by construing the transactions to be a public offering of bidder securities to the target shareholders. Rule 145.

Thus, the purchasing firm in a stock merger must file a 1933 Act registration statement with the SEC as well as a 1934 Act proxy statement. The registrant may choose to file the package confidentially. For statutory mergers and asset sales, a Form S-4 registration statement consists of the seller's proxy or information statement enclosed in the buyer's prospectus cover; the registration statement is a *wrap around* the proxy statement. A part of the Form S-4 thus also serves as a proxy statement for the target and, if necessary, the purchaser. If a purchasing firm, as issuer, uses a Form S-4 and incorporates by reference other public disclosure documents, the issuer must send the form at least 20 days in advance of the date of the shareholders' meeting. If the buyer does not want to assume liability for the seller's representations in its proxy statement or the buyer wants to narrow the 20-day notice requirement, then the buyer can register the transaction on a basic Form S-1 instead of a Form S-4, but Form S-1 does not permit liberal incorporation by reference of other 1934 Act reports, as does Form S-4, and thus is much more expensive to prepare and mail.

The purchasing firm may mail a preliminary prospectus to target shareholders but ordinarily will not because the purchasing firm cannot include a proxy card in the mailing. If the SEC staff decides to review and comment on the filing, all is delayed until the comments are resolved. Once the SEC declares the registration statement effective, the purchasing firm mails the combined final prospectus/definitive proxy statement along with a proxy card to all the selling firm shareholders.

If the target shareholders are already protected by the proxy solicitation rules of the 1934 Act, why do we need the additional set of disclosure requirements that attach to a registration statement under the 1933 Act? The real purpose of

Rule 145 is evident in subsections (c) and (d). The main effects of these sections are, first, to make *underwriters* of the target firm and its controlling officers and shareholders (as underwriters they are liable for disclosure violations under § 11 of the 1933 Act) and, second, to restrict the resale of securities obtained by target shareholders who control the target, so-called target affiliates (this group includes target managers as well as controlling shareholders). These resale requirements have a major impact on the willingness of target shareholders to vote for swap acquisitions, in which they take acquired securities for their target shares. Controlling target shareholders who are unwilling to hold securities in the acquired firm and want to cash out immediately after the acquisition will not agree to a swap.

Affiliates of the target can publicly resell their buyer firm securities only by registering the resale or by complying with the narrow resale restrictions in Rule 145(d), which incorporates by reference parts of Rule 144. The affiliates who choose to register their resales can *piggyback* their registration on the buyer's Form S-4 (a *secondary offering*). If the original Form S-4 does not mention the resales, the target affiliates can file a post-effective amendment to the buyer's form containing the prospectus (offering document) that the affiliates intend to use in the sales and other information on the identity of the sellers, the underwriting and distribution arrangements for the resales, the closing of the acquisition in which the shares were issued, and any material developments with respect to the combined firm subsequent to the closing. The affiliates cannot send the prospectus to offerees until the amendment becomes effective. Because the shares to be resold by the affiliates can be registered only by the *acquiring* firm, the target must bargain for a piggyback registration during the negotiations over the acquisition agreement and include registration rights in the agreement. Those rights normally include conditions on the length of time the buyer must keep the registration effective, the expiration of the registration right, the minimum number of shares to be registered, and the time of year at which registration may be requested.

In Rule 145(c) and (d), target shareholders in Rule 145 transactions reselling securities without use of a piggyback secondary offering in a 1933 Act registration statement fall into four categories. First, if the target shareholder is not an affiliate of the target and not an affiliate of the buyer, Rule 145(c) does not apply, and the resales are unrestricted. Second, if the target shareholder is an affiliate of the target and after the transaction is not an affiliate of the buyer, resales, to be protected, must comply with Rule 145(d)(1), (2) or (3). Third, if the target shareholder is an affiliate of the target and an affiliate of the buyer after the transaction, resales are protected only if in compliance with Rule 145(d)(1). And fourth, if the target shareholder is not an affiliate of the target and after the transaction becomes an affiliate of the buyer, Rule 145(c) does not apply, but § 2(11) and Rule 144 do, if no other exemption can be found.

In the usual case, a controlling party of the target takes stock in the buyer but does not become a controlling party in the buyer. The resale rules for this affiliate of the buyer but not the seller are as follows. Pursuant to Rule 145(d)(1), she may resell a limited amount of stock immediately—that is, without any holding period—if the acquiring company meets the current public information requirement of Rule 144(c), if the resales are effected in brokers' transactions, as defined by Rule 144(f) and (g), and if the resales do not during each three-month period exceed 1 percent of the total outstanding shares of the issuer (that is, the acquiring company) or the average weekly trading volume in the shares for the past four weeks. Rule 144(e). In addition, Rule 145(d)(2) permits unlimited resales after a one-year holding period, provided only that the issuer meets the current public information requirement of Rule 144(c). After a two-year holding period, Rule 145(d)(3) permits her to resell with no restrictions.

C. The Effect of the 1933 Act on Recapitalizations

The 1933 Act contains a special exemption from registration for securities distributed in voluntary exchanges and recapitalizations. The exemption is contained in § 3(a)(9) for "any security exchanged by the issuer with its existing security holders exclusively where no commission or other remuneration is paid or given directly or indirectly for soliciting such exchange."

Exchange transactions may occur in a wide variety of circumstances—for example, a conversion of bonds to stock or preferred stock to common stock. The exemption is quite narrow. The exemption is important for poison pill plans. Popular poison pill plans consist of rights distributed as dividends on the common stock. A rights or stock dividend is not a sale and does not require registration under the 1933 Act. The issuer of both securities must be identical; no part of the offering may be made to anyone other than existing security holders; and the firm cannot pay anyone for soliciting proxies.

§ 25. The Disclosure Requirements of Federal Securities Law

A. Introduction to Mandatory Disclosure Requirements in Federal Securities Law

In the United States, the disclosure obligation of publicly-traded firms is defined from the ground up by the accumulation of a constantly growing body of specific federal rules. The aggregate effect of the federal rules constitutes our mandatory disclosure system. There are other sources of disclosure obligations for publicly-traded firms. Most state corporate codes include minimal disclosure obligations, e.g., MBCA § 16.20 (requiring annual

reports to shareholders), as does Delaware case
law, which affects over one-half of our NYSE companies. E.g., *Marhart v. Calmat* (Del. Ch. 1992).
And our organized stock trading markets include
disclosure obligations in their private listing
contracts. But the details of the Securities and
Exchange Act of 1934, now heavily laden with (and
even, in some cases, superseded by) a thick
clothing of SEC administrative rules, are the
dominant source of disclosure obligations for our
publicly-traded companies.

The SEC rules, adopted through the formal
procedures of the Administrative Procedure Act,
have the force of law and are themselves multi-
layered. They come in the form of *Regulations*,
which contain individual *Rules*, which refer to
Forms or *Schedules*, which contain *Items* (which
often cross-reference other Schedules). SEC pronouncements on how to interpret the rules in light
of specific facts come in *Interpretive Releases*, *No-
Action Letters*, agency enforcement proceedings,
and *amicus* briefs filed with federal courts and
miscellaneous public comments by agency officials.

No General Duty to Disclose. In the United
States there is no general overarching legal duty to
disclose material facts, plans, strategies or other
information to the trading markets. The Supreme
Court articulated the principle in 1980: A duty to
disclose "does not arise from the mere possession of
non-public information...when an allegation of
fraud is based upon nondisclosure, there can be no

fraud absent a duty to speak." *Chiarella v. United States* (U.S. 1980). A precise formulation of when the duty to speak arises under federal law is hazardous, however. One reasonable classification of the duty to speak could be the following.

A duty to speak arises in two contexts, the second of which is, to some degree, under the control of the issuer. First, the 1934 Act, as heavily supplemented by SEC Regulations, requires publicly-traded firms to file periodic reports, annual reports and quarterly reports. The 1934 Act requires an issuer to file annual reports on Form 10-K, which must contain a full analysis of the issuer's business, audited financial statements, disclosures on pending legal proceedings, and a management discussion and analysis (MD&A) section. The 1934 Act also requires issuers to file quarterly reports on Form 10-Q. All publicly-traded firms, whether or not they solicit proxies, are also required to send a proxy statement to their shareholders in anticipation of the firm's required annual meeting. Exchange Act § 14(c); Reg. 14C.

Second, an issuer must file public reports with the SEC on the occurrence of specified events. Major corporate transactions (mergers and recapitalizations, for example) require a current report on Form 8-K. The events include changes in control of the issuer, acquisition or disposition of assets, bankruptcy or receivership, changes in the issuer's certifying accountant, and any resignation of the issuer's directors. The form does not require the disclosure of changes in operating results, such as sale figures or revenue trends. There are specific SEC rules that detail disclosure requirements for firms that call special shareholder meetings, announce a tender offer, respond to a tender offer, repurchase shares to go private or in response to a tender offer, make a public offering of securities, or purchase over 5 percent of the registered stock of another firm. Federal judges have held, using the open-textured SEC Rule 10b-5, that share repurchases or the existence of rumors affecting stock price that are attributable to the leaks or trades of insiders trigger a firm's obligation to disclose all material information on the firm's affairs. E.g., *Elkind v. Liggett & Myers, Inc.* (2d Cir. 1980).

If a firm chooses to speak to the trading markets, that is, federal law does not require the statement, Rule 10b-5 applies nonetheless to require that the statement be sufficiently complete so as to not mislead. Some refer to the statements in this category as *voluntary statements*. This duty to be complete is a subset of, in essence, a third category of mandatory disclosure obligation often called the *half-truth rule*.

The Duty Not to Publish Half-Truths. Whenever a duty to speak attaches, usually as the result of an obligation to file reports with the SEC pursuant to a specific administrative regulation or schedule, an issuer must first satisfy the subject matter requirements of whatever statute, rule, regulation or schedule is appropriate. The specific information requested is presumed material. In addition, the firm must satisfy a general obligation, known among securities practitioners as the *half-truth* rule, to "add [ ] such further material information, if any, as may be necessary to make the required statements, in the light of the circumstances under which they are made not misleading." SEC Rule 10b-5. In other words, a half-truth, a partial disclosure of facts that are literally correct but misleading in light of facts that are concealed, is as culpable as an affirmative misrepresentation. A definition of materiality is crucial to the doctrine.

The half-truth rule appears in other contexts defined by case law precedent as well. If the duty to speak arises from case law under Rule 10b-5 or a similar general antifraud rule, a firm must disclose all material information with any other information necessary to make the information disclosed not misleading. Thus a firm, when obliged to correct market rumors originating with statements or trades by insiders, for example, must disclose information sufficient to satisfy the half-truth rule. If the duty to speak is triggered by a firm's voluntary statements, the statements must be truthful and supplemented by other information necessary to make the statements not misleading.

Courts have long recognized that the half-truth rule when applied to SEC forms or schedules cannot be pressed to its literal boundaries. In the context of specific disclosure schedules, the half-truth doctrine, if read literally, could require an issuer to supplement any schedule with all facts on the issuer material to investors regardless of the specific, identified items of information required by the schedule. In theory, any non-public material information, although not covered by a specific item in a form or schedule, could, if disclosed, make a given annual or quarterly report, in a sense, more accurate or more complete and not misleading. If the half-truth rule is so understood, all SEC required filings, whether periodic reports or event-triggered reports, would be expanded into occasions for a disclosure of all material facts. Courts seem to limit the doctrine to one requiring a disclosure only of facts that specifically contradict the statements in forms or schedules (or in press releases) rather than one requiring the issuer "to state every fact about stock offered that a prospective purchaser might like to know or that might, if known, tend to influence his decision." E.g., *Otis & Co. v. SEC* (6th Cir. 1939). See also *Lewis v. Chrysler Corp.* (3d Cir. 1991). Information, for example, that relates only to quantification, the gravity or significance of a public statement, apparently does not have to be disclosed. *Backman v. Polaroid Corp.* (1st Cir. 1990).

On the other hand, there is a class of cases in which the courts do appear to put a broad gloss on the half-truth obligation. The federal courts do read the half-truth language broadly if the duty to speak is triggered by firm or insider trading under SEC Rule 10b-5. In such cases, all material information on the firm must be available to third parties on the opposite side of the trade. Here the firm's option is not to trade, or to disclose fully in the context of a trade. The distinction makes sense. The ease of avoiding the disclosure obligation entirely (by not trading) is not replicated when a firm owes the SEC a periodic report, for example.

Materiality. The Supreme Court penned the definition of materiality in *TSC Industries, Inc. v. Northway, Inc.* (U.S. 1976):

An omitted fact is material if there is a substantial likelihood that a reasonable share-holder would consider it important in deciding how to vote.... It does not require proof of a substantial likelihood that disclosure of the omitted fact would have caused the reasonable investor to change his vote. What the standard does contemplate is a showing of a substantial likelihood that, under all the circumstances, the omitted fact would have assumed actual significance in the deliberations of the reasonable shareholder. Put another way, there must be a substantial likelihood that the disclosure of the omitted fact would have been viewed by the reasonable investor as having significantly altered the "total mix" of information made available....

Federal circuit courts have supplemented the definition by categorizing as immaterial generalized statements of optimism ("mere puffing") and statements qualified with specific risk disclosures or other cautionary statements. E.g., *Grossman v. Novell* (10th Cir. 1997). The circuit courts are split, however, over whether internal financial projections (and their cousins, asset appraisals) are material. E.g., *Walker v. Action Indus.* (4th Cir. 1987) (no, disagreeing with the Third, Seventh, Sixth and Ninth Circuits and following the Second Circuit).

B. Projections of Acquisition Success

It goes almost without saying that projections are an important part of all acquisitions. Participants negotiating an acquisition are necessarily projecting the post-acquisition value of a combined firm and comparing this figure with projections of the value of the constituent firms standing alone. The SEC knows that shareholders view the projections as significant but fears that managers will misuse them and shareholders will misunderstand them (that is, overrate their importance). Moreover, the SEC is concerned that managers' misuse of projections would be difficult to police. A projection is only an opinion of future events, usually heavily qualified.

Known as the debate over *prospective* or *forward-looking* information, the SEC has recently been very active on the issue. Under the SEC rules and interpretative releases, there are four categories of projections: predictions an issuer *must* create and disclose; predictions an issuer must disclose *if* created and available; predictions an issuer *can voluntarily* disclose, if in good faith and with a reasonable basis in fact; and finally, predictions an issuer *cannot* legally disclose even if created and available. As a result of the SEC's traditional suspicion of predictions, most lawyers advise their clients not to disclose predictions unless legally required to do so.

1. SEC Forms and Schedules: Required Projections of Post-Acquisition Performance

Shareholder Voting and the Proxy Statement. There are three separate bits of language in the Schedule 14A that appear to call for the disclosure of prospective information. Item 14, for example, calls for financial statements meeting the requirements of Article 11 of Regulation S-X. Article 11 requires pro forma financial information if significant business combinations are *probable*. In essence, the pro forma financials present the combined financials of the two constituent corporations as if they had combined on the date of the last financial statements prepared by the surviving company. Thus, in a sense, the information is not prospective at all, it is historical in that the companies are combined as of a past date.

At issue, however, are the obligations of the firms in an acquisition to adjust or footnote the pro forma financials if the pro formas do not accurately reflect what is likely to occur in the transaction. The SEC regulations on Article 11 contain some general language on the matter, requiring that pro formas be adjusted in light of the structure of any planned acquisition "to give effect to the range of possible results." SEC Reg. § 210.11-02(b)(8). These adjustments and, in lieu thereof, the footnotes to the pro forma *could* constitute a very valuable kind of prospective information for investors. Yet accountants read this language in Article 11 very narrowly. The dominant footnote to pro formas is a disclaimer. The disclaimer states that the pro formas are a "mechanical exercise": They are not an accurate indication of any real results in the acquisition, and they do not include any quantification of synergy gains and other savings that may occur in the acquisition.

Article 11 also has a little-used provision that allows a firm, if it so chooses, to file a financial forecast *in lieu of* a pro forma. The forecast is a condensed statement under SEC Reg. § 210.11-03. The financial forecast must cover a period at least 12 months after the estimated consummation date of the transaction and set out clearly "assumptions particularly relevant to the transaction and effects thereof." Id. Although forecasts are very carefully regulated by generally accepted accounting principles, professional standards generated by accountants themselves, there is room in such forecasts to make predictions about the future results of an acquisition. In practice, accountants often advise firms not to use the forecast rule.

A second call for prospective information in Item 14 appears to be the language in subsection (a)(3)(ii) asking for "the reasons for engaging in the transaction." A calculation of the potential synergy gains in an acquisition would appear to be a reason. In practice, however, parties meet the language by disclosing only a very general laundry list of reasons; there is no quantification nor any ranking of reasons included in the list. Item 14(a)(10) comes the closest to asking for some concrete estimates: "If a report, opinion or apprais-al materially relating to the transaction has been received from an outside party, and such report, opinion or appraisal is referred to in the proxy statement, furnish the same...." The requirement is readily avoidable, however. Parties to the trans-action usually omit any reference to opinions and appraisal, even if available, in their proxy information statements.

A third call for prospective information appears in the tame language of Item 303(a) in Regulation S-K. Item 303 of Regulation S-K is incorporated by reference in Items 12 and 14 of Regulation 14A. The instruction deals with the "Management's Discussion and Analysis" (MD&A) section of a firm's financial statements. The MD&A is text that helps readers understand the bare numbers in the financials themselves. Instruction 3 requires that "the discussion and analysis shall focus specifically on material events and uncertainties known to management that would cause reported financial information not to be necessarily indicative of future operating results." Instruction 7 to Item 303(a) requires the disclosure of "presently known data which will impact upon future operating results."

The SEC has defined "required prospective information" as "currently known trends, events, and uncertainties that are reasonably expected to have material effects" and has defined "optional forward-looking information" as involving "anticipating a future trend or event or anticipating a less predictable impact of a known event, trend or uncertainty." SEC Rel. No. 6711 (April 24, 1987), 52 F.R. 13717. The Commission has attempted to give additional substance to the hazy distinction between prospective information that an issuer must disclose and forward-looking information that an issuer may disclose through a series of double negatives. Fin. Rep. Rel. 36, SEC Rel. No. 6835; Exch. Act Rel. No. 26831 (May 18, 1989). First, management must determine whether the known trend or event is likely to occur. If management determines that it is not reasonably likely to occur, no disclosure is required. Second, if management cannot make a determination that the event is not likely to occur, disclosure is required unless management determines that a material effect on the financial condition of the reporting company is not reasonably likely to occur.

Stock Swaps and the Prospectus. Purchasing firms issuing securities as consideration in stock-for-stock mergers, stock-for-assets asset acquisitions or stock-for-stock tender offers are selling securities for the purposes of the Securities Act of 1933. SEC Rule 145. If a purchasing firm cannot qualify under an exemption, the firm must register the securities with the SEC and distribute the securities using a selling document entitled a *prospectus.* The form follows the pattern established in the proxy regulations noted above. For example, Item 3(e) and (f) incorporates Item 301 of Regulation S-K and requires pro forma information on book value per share, cash dividends, and income per share, assuming the acquisition. Item 4 incorporates by reference Article 11 of Regulation S-X and requires pro forma financial statements. Item 303 of Regulation S-K on MD&A text applies as well. E.g., Item 12(b)(3)(v); Item 13(a)(3)(v); Item 14(h). Item 4(b) notes that "if a report, opinion or appraisal materially relating to the transaction has been received from an outside party, and such report, opinion, or appraisal is referred to in the prospectus...," the issuer must include information on the details of the report.

Tender Offers and Schedules TO, 13E-3 and 14d-9. Schedule TO, the offerors' announcing document, and Schedule 14d-9, the targets' response, also follow the pattern discussed above for proxy statements requiring pro forma financials and a disclosure of known trends in the MD&A language. In addition, however, Schedule TO, Item 6 requires a bidder to state the purposes of the tender offer including any plans, proposals or negotiations that relate to or would result in a follow-up merger (a squeeze-out, for example), the subsequent sale of the target's assets (a bust-up, for example), any change in the board or management of the target, any change in the capitalization or dividend policy, any material change in corporate structure, and any plans to delist the target's securities from a national stock exchange. Schedule TO covers issuer stock repurchases in tender offers as well.

A series of novel provisions apply to the going-private transaction, however. Item 8 in Schedule 13E-3 requires a statement on the fairness of the transaction by the issuer. The item also requires reasonable detail on the material factors behind the statement and the weight assigned to each factor. Item 9 supplements Item 8 and requires that an issuer *must* disclose any report, opinion or appraisal from an outside party (other than an opinion of counsel—fairness opinions from investment bankers, for example) that is materially related to the transaction, including those relating to the fairness of the consideration and those relating to the fairness of the transaction.

Targets in third-party tender offers must state reasons for whatever recommendation they make to their shareholders in response to a tender offer (Schedule 14d-9, Item 4), and must disclose negotiations with other potential acquirors in Item 7. If the target has signed an agreement in principle with another acquiror, the target must disclose the details of the acquisition, including the acquiror's future plans for the target.

2. SEC Rules on Permission to Make Voluntary Projections of Post-Acquisition Performance

If disclosure is not required, issuers can decide to disclose forward-looking information anyway. Rule 175 and Rule 3b-6 permit a firm to disclose a short, specific list of projections in required annual or quarterly reports. The SEC terms the disclosures *forward-looking information*. Rule 175 allows, for example, projections of "revenues, income (loss), earnings (loss) per share, capital expenditures, dividends, capital structure or other financial items" and "a statement of management's plans and objectives for future operations." Presumably each type of projection could be made about the business future of a surviving entity in an acquisition or reorganization. The safe harbor rules protect an issuer's voluntary projections only if made with a reasonable basis and in good faith.

The Rules do not specifically require the disclosure of the assumptions that underlie the forward-looking statements, but the SEC takes the position that

> under certain circumstances the disclosure of the assumptions may be material to an understanding of the projected results...and key

assumptions underlying a forward looking statement are of such significance that their disclosure may be necessary in order for the statement to meet the reasonable basis and good faith standards embodied in the rule.

Safe Harbor Rule for Projections, Sec. Act Rel. No. 6084 (July 5, 1979).

Rule 175 and Rule 3b-6 do not include and, therefore, do not protect projections of future stock prices or other market values of the survivor—the information probably most desired by selling firm shareholders who are deciding whether to vote on a transaction that will exchange their shares for stock in the survivor. See also Sec. Exch. Act § 21E(i)(1). Indeed, SEC Rule 14a-9, the general anti-fraud rule applicable to proxy statements, in its list of examples of projections that may be misleading, includes "predictions as to specific future market values." The SEC is generally very suspicious of broad predictions by firm managers on post-acquisition stock prices, believing that given half a chance, managers will imitate snake oil salesmen. The SEC fears that managers will mislead their shareholders with general exaggerated claims that are not susceptible to correction by after-the-fact litigation based on fraud.

The definition of forward-looking information in the Rules was incorporated by Congress into the safe harbor provisions of the Private Litigation Reform Act of 1995. Under the provisions, forward-looking statements are not fraudulent in the context of private civil actions (the exclusion does not apply to the SEC's prosecutions) if they are "accompanied by meaningful cautionary statements identifying important factors that could cause actual results to differ materially from those in the forward looking statement" or if the plaintiff fails to prove actual knowledge that a statement is false or misleading. Sec. Act of 1933, § 27A(c)(1); Sec. Exch. Act of 1934, § 21E(c)(1). The Act does not apply to tender offer disclosures, however. The SEC provisions that allow but do not require disclosure of certain types of prospective information are largely unused, as lawyers counsel their client to disclose only that which is required and even then only at minimal levels.

3. The Duty to Amend, Correct or Update Projections

The *duty to amend* is found expressly in several of the disclosure schedules pertaining to stock acquisitions. Rule 13d-2, for example, requires a promptly filed amendment for any material changes in the facts disclosed in an original filing. The duty to amend is an express direction to amend in the schedules, forms and rules. See also Rules 14d-6(d), 14d-9(b), 13e-3(e)(2) and 13e-4(e)(2). The *duty to correct* is the obligation of a filing company to correct promptly statements that it discovers were incorrect when made. See, e.g., *Ross v. A.H. Robbins Co.* (S.D.N.Y. 1979). The *duty to update*, the most controversial of the three, is a general duty derived from Rule 10b-5 to supplement statements (even when there is otherwise no specific duty to amend) that were accurate when made but that have become inaccurate or misleading due to subsequent events. The duty to update attaches to forward-looking statements only (explicit firm projections and predictions made in the public filings or statements). There is disagreement among the federal circuit courts on whether the duty exists at all—the Seventh Circuit says no, the First, Second and Third Circuit Courts say yes. *Stransky v. Summins Engine Co.* (7th Cir. 1995); *Weiner v. Quaker Oats Co.* (3d Cir. 1997); *In re Time Warner Inc.* (2d Cir. 1993); *Backman v. Polaroid* (1st Cir. 1990).

C. The Duty to Disclose Acquisition Negotiations

When must a firm disclose the existence of preliminary merger negotiations? The answer depends on whether the firm is under an obligation to file a periodic report (a 10-K or 10-Q) or an episodic report (a registration statement). If so, the forms each contain an explicit anti-half-truth rule (the firm must disclose whatever is necessary so the required disclosures are not misleading). The materiality standard announced in *Basic v. Levinson* (U.S. 1988), for similar language in Rule 10b-5 would seem to apply. The standard is a "balancing of both the indicated probability that the event will occur and the anticipated magnitude of the event in light of the totality of the company activity." Since major acquisitions are always big news, a large acquisition may be material even if the probability of it occurring is less than 50 percent.

The periodic reporting forms also incorporate by reference Regulation S-X. Regulation S-X contains Item 303 requiring MD&A statements on *known events* that could also require disclosure of the negotiations. The SEC, in Release 33-6835, has confused the issue by construing Item 303 to allow parties to stay quiet if disclosure "would jeopardize completion of the transaction." Otherwise, when the negotiations (as known events) are reasonably likely to have material effects on a firm, the firm must disclose them. In the release the SEC defers to Form 8-K, requiring reporting of extraordinary events, which requires disclosure of acquisitions only on the completion of the acquisition. It is not clear whether the reservations in the release apply also to the anti-half-truth language in the reporting schedules.

If no periodic reports need to be filed, is there a general disclosure obligation for material preliminary merger discussions? *Basic* is not on point. At issue in *Basic* was the materiality of *voluntarily made* disclosures, press releases and comments to the NYSE that were admittedly false. If the statements were material, Rule 10b-5 would apply without question. To define materiality, the Court adopted a modified version of the materiality standard first articulated in *Texas Gulf Sulphur* (significance of deal times its probability of occurrence) and rejected the bright-line test of *Greenfield* (when parties reach an agreement in principle on the major terms).

Only in dicta (in footnote 17) does the Court in *Basic* address the issue of whether Rule 10b-5 itself imposed a general duty to speak, and then only obliquely. Most lawyers understand that the case gives a negative answer to the question, however. As understood, the case establishes that Rule 10b-5, by itself, does not establish a general disclosure obligation for preliminary merger discussions. In footnote 17, the Court penned the now often-quoted phrase: "[S]ilence, absent a duty to disclose, is not misleading." This phrase leads lawyers to believe that there is no general duty to disclose even admittedly material events. The Court also noted that a "no comment" was "generally" the same as silence.

There are two significant caveats to the general rule, however. First, the *Weiner* case from the Third Circuit throws a significant wrench in the analysis using a broad form of a duty to update that requires an early disclosure of merger discussions (a firm must update outstanding public filings and public statements). *Weiner v. Quaker Oats Co.* (3d Cir. 1997). Several other circuits do not and will follow *Weiner*, however. Second, in contrast to the requirements of Rule 10b-5 as interpreted in *Basic*, the NYSE listing requirements give a clear positive answer. In

NYSE Listing Company Manual § 202.05, the exchange requires of listed companies that, if the information is likely to affect trading prices (most preliminary merger discussions, once discovered, do affect price), it must be disclosed to the exchange. Section 202.50 is buttressed by § 202.01 that requires disclosure whenever leaks of sensitive information are likely and by § 202.03 that requires disclosure whenever the trading price shows unusual volatility.

D. Disclosing Stock Purchases of 5 Percent or Greater: Section 13(d) of the Williams Act

Section 13(d) of the SEA is a portion of the 1967 Williams Act. The statute applies to the acquisition of voting stock of publicly-traded companies. Once a purchaser "with an intent to control" acquires over 5 percent of the stock, it has 10 days in which to file a public disclosure statement, Schedule 13D. Purchasers buy 4.99 percent at their leisure and then race to buy as much as they can in 10 days (a bidder worth its salt can usually get up to 10 or 11 percent) before they file. If a purchaser has no "intent to control" it files a Schedule 13G by February 15 of the following year. Schedule 13D, in Item 4, requires the disclosure of source of funds and purposes, plans or proposals. Those who cheat try to warehouse stock in phony accounts to avoid an early disclosure. Ivan Boesky pled guilty and went to jail primarily on § 13(d) violations.

The *Rondeau v. Mosinee Paper Corp.* (U.S. 1975) case explains the good intentions behind the section, shows how it can catch novice bidders unaware and deals with the question of remedy. The seller wanted the stock held by a purchaser who had violated the section "sterilized" (stripped of voting power). The Court of Appeals, ever vigilant, agreed but the Supreme Court reversed (over Justice Douglas's dissent). Rondeau, the purchaser, had cured, the shareholders had the required information, and Rondeau had made no further efforts at control. The Court noted the limited scope of the holding and also reserved the question of whether shareholders, who sold cheap during the period after which disclosure was required and was not made, could sue.

The § 13(d) fairness rule does have negative consequences. It deters some buyers at the margin by increasing the costs of purchasing control. How would one purchase control without the rule? The cheapest way is usually through, first, quiet toe-hold purchases (negotiated private purchases and open-market purchases) until rumors flood the market; second, a public tender offer for legal control; and, third, a back-end cash-out merger. Why does a public tender offer at some point become cheaper than more negotiated or open-market purchases? A flat price retards the tendency to hoard or hold out when rumors about a takeover are abundant. Early disclosure increases costs.

In the eighties, § 13(d) empowered managers to defend their firms. Now that a scorched earth defense is no longer fashionable (target boards understand their obligation to sell the firm), the section now empowers managers to negotiate for a higher price from the bidder (to seek a second, higher bidder). At issue is whether target shareholders would vote to put the rule in all stock contracts if there was no § 13(d). The shareholders would make a trade-off of fewer potential bidders against a higher price on bids that do occur.

Critics also question why passive shareholders of a firm have access to information created by a stranger to the firm (the bidder). There is no fiduciary duty of stranger to shareholders; the stranger is not using firm assets and does not have insider information (it developed its own information at considerable expense); and the shareholders have done nothing other than to elect the old managers, which may be the problem. Why, critics ask, is it fair to force those who develop information, create value, to give it away for nothing? The rule discourages those who would otherwise develop valuable information on target firm value.

CHAPTER 7

ACCOUNTING ISSUES IN MERGERS AND ACQUISITIONS

In this discussion the acquiring company will be referred to as "acquirer" and the acquired company will be called "target." In the case of an outright sale of the business assets of target, it may not survive after the transaction closes, so the focus will shift solely to acquirer. If acquirer acquires an interest in the stock of target, acquirer's shareholders will be interested in the impact of the acquisition of target on acquirer's profitability— does the deal have an "accretive effect" on earnings? If target is merged into acquirer through a reorganization, target's continuing financial results become part of those for acquirer. Consequently, the financial accounting aspects of mergers and acquisitions usually focus on the post-acquisition impact on acquirer.

§ 26. Sources of Financial Accounting Principles

Managerial accounting focuses on information produced for internal use in varied contexts such as pricing, budgeting and inventory planning. In comparison, *financial accounting* reports the overall financial position of the enterprise at certain points in time (for example, quarterly or annually), and the information is relied upon primarily by external users such as lenders, labor unions, regulators, investment analysts and investors. One of those financial accounting measures discussed below, *earnings per share*, is used in evaluating the profitability impacts of merger and acquisition transactions. Another measure of enterprise profitability used by analysts is so-called "EBITDA," an acronym for a cash flow measure derived from financial accounting earnings, but before interest, tax, depreciation, and amortization expenses. Financial accounting information provides the foundations of such analyses, and therefore is the focus of this chapter.

Financial accounting information must be *reliable*, accurately and neutrally reflecting the underlying transactions of the enterprise. To ensure reliability, management must adopt appropriate internal control and reporting systems. Accounting information must also be *relevant*, capable of making a difference in decisions by potential users of the information. Financial accounting information should be reported in a *consistent* manner from reporting period to reporting period. Furthermore, financial accounting information should be based on common principles that make the basis for the information *comparable* from enterprise to enterprise. In that regard, reference is frequently made to *generally accepted accounting principles* or *GAAP*. In the United States GAAP has been largely determined by the private sector (principally the accounting profession) through pronouncements of the Financial Accounting Standards Board ("FASB") (a non-profit organization comprised of members from professional accounting firms, as well as industry) and its predecessor, the Accounting Principles Board ("APB"), created by the American Institute of Certified Public Accountants. However, for publicly-traded companies the Securities and Exchange Commission ("SEC"), principally through the Office of the Chief Accountant, works with the accounting profession and the FASB to develop accounting standards for reporting companies. While the SEC has statutory authority to prescribe the accounting principles utilized in reports filed with it, it has generally relied on the accounting profession to develop such rules. However, in some areas, most notably Regulation S-X, the SEC has specified the type of financial information that must be supplied by a reporting company.

§ 27. The Basic Financial Accounting Statements

The basic financial statements for an enterprise include: (1) an *earnings statement* (income statement or profit and loss statement) which reflects operating performance of the enterprise for a specific period of time, generally a quarter or year; (2) a *balance sheet* (or statement of financial position) which reflects the assets, liabilities, and owners' equity of the enterprise as of a specific point in time; and (3) a *statement of cash flows* which reflects the cash inflows and outflows of the enterprise for the period.

Earnings per share, a fundamental driver of share price, is computed from the income statement by dividing the earnings of the enterprise by the number of outstanding (or deemed outstanding for options and convertible securities under complicated "dilution" rules) shares. The *income statement* has been compared to a motion picture of an enterprise's activities over the reporting period, accumulating the results of the sales of its goods or services and subtracting the matching costs of goods sold, overhead (such as wages and salaries, rent, supplies and depreciation), interest expense, and taxes. The income statement can be misleading if accepted at face value. First, it reports past results and is of limited aid in forecasting future profitability. Indeed, with a fast-growing company the focus of analysts in predicting the future price of a stock is often not on "trailing" earnings but rather on future earnings. Second, the income statement can report non-cash expenditures (such as depreciation of buildings and equipment) that decrease earnings but not cash flow (hence the usefulness of EBITDA analysis discussed above). Third, it would be rare for a public company to report on a simple cash receipts-and-expenditures basis. Consequently the accrual method of accounting is employed, and it permits some latitude (and potential abuses) in the timing of revenue recognition and the deduction of costs.

The *balance sheet* accumulates, with some exceptions, the historical "book" accounting value of assets, subtracting liabilities to arrive at the equity or net worth of the enterprise. Like the income statement, the balance sheet can present information that is potentially misleading. First— with some exceptions for cash, accounts receivable, and marketable securities—historic cost, rather than current fair value, is reported for assets. In a declining industry book value may overstate the value of assets. On the other hand, for assets purchased long ago the book value may understate the current fair value. Second, the balance sheet amounts may not include valuable assets, such as internally developed goodwill, going concern value, or important innovations, or may exclude liabilities such as certain lease obligations, substituting footnote disclosures that are consequently a critical part of the financial statements.

The *statement of cash flows* (once referred to as the statement of changes in financial position, the sources and uses of financial resources statement, or the funds statement) presents changes in an enterprise's financial position that are normally generated from operations and summarizes the financing and investing activities of the enterprise for the same period. The statement *adds* the balance of cash and cash equivalents (such as short-term, highly liquid investments) at the beginning of the year, cash generated from operations, cash raised from the issuance of debt or equity, and cash raised from the sale of fixed assets, and *subtracts* dividend distributions, cash paid in redemption of debt or stock, and the cash acquisition of fixed assets. The net result of the computation should equal the ending balance of cash and cash equivalents at the end of the year. An enterprise with a number of non-cash expenditures may report insubstantial earnings while enjoying a robust cash flow. On the other hand, a net profit on the income statement may not, due to income recognition conventions that report the income in advance of the receipt of payment, be accompanied by a positive cash flow, a condition that may not be sustainable for the long-term.

§ 28. Acquisition Accounting: The Cost Method—Acquisitions of Less Than 20 Percent of Target's Outstanding Common Stock

Acquirer may acquire less than 20 percent of target's outstanding common stock. Two principal financial accounting issues arise: (1) When and how should acquirer's income statement reflect the earnings of target? (2) How should acquirer's balance sheet reflect the investment in target?

With respect to the first issue, under the *cost method* of accounting, the separate accounting identity of target is respected and acquirer reports income from target's operations only when and if dividends are distributed by target to acquirer. Dividends from target in excess of its earnings subsequent to the acquisition date are a return of acquirer's investment and reduce the reported amount of the investment. When acquirer sells the stock of target, acquirer will record as gain or loss on its income statement, the difference between the cost basis of the investment (as adjusted for any dividends in excess of earnings) and its sales price. However, as discussed in the following paragraphs, unrealized holding gains and losses of certain equity securities must also be included in current earnings.

With respect to the second issue of balance sheet presentation, the accounting nomenclature for the investment is determinative. FASB Statement 115, "Accounting for Certain Investments in Debt and Equity Securities," characterizes equity securities that are bought and held principally for the purpose of selling them in the near term as *trading securities*. Trading is the active and frequent buying and selling of securities with the objective of producing profits on short-term differences in price. Equity investments that are not classified as trading securities are *available-for-sale* securities, and most strategic investments in companies like target would fall into this category unless a greater stake in target is acquired (FAS 115 does not apply to investments in equity securities accounted for under the equity method of accounting discussed below nor to investments in consolidated subsidiaries; those treatments are triggered by greater stakes held by acquirer in target). However, FAS 115 does not apply to investments in equity securities unless the fair value is *readily determinable*, with reference to bid-and-asked quotations that are currently available on a securities exchange registered with the SEC or in the over-the-counter market. FAS 115 might not therefore govern venture capital investments in closely-held companies and partnerships. Furthermore, equity securities for which sale is restricted by governmental (e.g., SEC Rule 144) or contractual requirement (other than in connection with a pledge as collateral) are not considered to have a readily determinable fair value unless the requirement terminates within one year or if the holder has the power to cause the requirement to be met within one year. Finally, this discussion is limited to *equity* securities. While warrants, rights and options can be considered an equity security, FAS 115 generally excludes convertible debt or redeemable/puttable preferred stock from that definition.

Once the FAS 115 categories are determined, the rest of the accounting treatment falls into place.

Excluded Investments. If FAS 115 does not apply to an equity investment, it is reported on the balance sheet at the original acquisition cost with adjustment only for other than temporary impairment of value (e.g., a series of operating losses of an investee or other factors may indicate that a decrease in value has occurred which is other than temporary and should be recognized).

Trading Securities. Under FAS 115, trading securities are classified as current assets on the balance sheet. Unrealized holding gains and losses are included in current earnings.

Available-for-Sale Securities. Under FAS 115, available-for-sale securities are classified as either current or noncurrent assets. If the investment in target is a marketable security representing the investment of cash available for current operations (assuming it is not already characterized as a trading security), the stock would be classified as a current asset. In the more likely case of a strategic investment in target, the stock would be classified as a noncurrent asset. Dividend income, as well as realized gains and losses, are included in earnings. Unrealized holding gains and losses are generally excluded from earnings, but reported as a separate component of shareholders' equity until realized. If an available-for-sale security suffers a decline in fair value below cost that is other than temporary, the cost basis is written down to fair value, and the amount of the write-down is included in earnings, accounted for as a realized loss. Subsequent increases in the fair value do not increase the previously written-down cost basis and are included in the separate component of shareholders' equity. Subsequent decreases in fair value, if temporary, are also included in the separate component of shareholders' equity.

§ 29. Acquisition Accounting: The Equity Method—Acquisitions of 20 to 50 Percent of Target's Outstanding Stock

APB Opinion 18 discusses the *equity method* of accounting, which is to be applied if acquirer is able to exercise significant influence over the operating and financial policies of target. While 20 percent or greater ownership produces a presumption of influence (and influence is presumed not to exist for ownership of less than 20 percent), both presumptions may be overcome by predominant evidence to the contrary.

If the equity method applies, acquirer records an investment in the stock of target at cost, but subsequently increases or decreases that investment by acquirer's share of the earnings or losses of target arising after the date of acquisition. Acquirer reports its share of the earnings or losses of target when and as earned by target, irrespective of whether or when dividend distributions are received. Dividends received from target are not income, but reduce the amount of the investment account. A comparison of the fair value of target's assets and the purchase price paid by acquirer can suggest the presence of goodwill. APB Opinion 18 previously required acquirer to reduce the reported share of earnings from target by a further adjustment for amortized goodwill (the concept of "amortizing" goodwill or other intangible assets is explained in the next section). However, FASB Statement 142, "Goodwill and Other Intangible Assets," issued in July 2001, provides that such goodwill should not be amortized, nor should the goodwill be tested for "impairment" under the principles of FAS 142 (discussed in the next section). Instead, the equity method investment remains subject to APB Opinion 18, requiring that a loss in value of an investment which is other than a temporary decline should be recognized the same as a loss in value of other long-term assets.

If the business of target is profitable, and acquirer's share of the profits exceeds dividend distributions, acquirer's reported investment in target will grow and exceed its cost. On the other hand, losses of target have an immediate impact on acquirer's income statement. The potential accounting impact on acquirer's reported profits may therefore influence the size of the planned stake in target.

§ 30. Acquisition Accounting: Acquisitions of Greater Than 50 Percent of the Stock of Another

If acquirer owns more than 50 percent of target, control of target is assumed (with target referred to as a *subsidiary*) and it is required that the accounting results of both companies be consolidated as one (FAS 94, "Consolidation of All Majority-Owned Subsidiaries"). Additional considerations in accounting for target's assets are discussed in the pages that follow.

A. Fundamentals of Purchase Accounting

In July 2001, the FASB issued two statements impacting 50 percent or more acquisitions (FASB Statement 141, "Business Combinations" and FASB Statement 142, "Goodwill and Other Intangible Assets"). In FAS 141, the FASB ruled that only the *purchase method* of accounting is permitted for business combinations initiated after June 30, 2001.

Under *purchase accounting*, the acquisition of target is treated as an arm's-length purchase of target by acquirer, reflecting the market values of the acquired assets and liabilities. The market values allocated to the acquired assets and liabilities are the basis for accounting in the future and are reported on acquirer's balance sheet— target's book values are not relevant. The lack of symmetry is remarkable in that the other assets and liabilities of acquirer remain at historical cost amounts and are not adjusted to reflect their market values; this is why it is so critical to have principles for determining which of the two combining companies is the acquirer. Consequently, all pertinent facts are examined in determining which party is considered to be the acquirer, including relative voting power in the combined enterprise, composition of the board of directors and senior management, and which company received a premium as an inducement for the combination. The income statements of acquirer reflect only the post-acquisition earnings of target. If acquirer is acquiring target for a premium price, the purchase price in excess of the amounts assigned to target's identifiable assets will be ascribed to goodwill. On the other hand, if acquirer acquires the assets at a bargain price, below target's historical cost, the "negative goodwill" is eliminated by reducing the historical cost of certain classes of target's assets, to zero if necessary, with any remaining goodwill reported as an extraordinary gain.

Amortization is the expensing of a portion of the value listed on the firm's balance sheet of an intangible asset (an asset that lacks physical substance) with a limited useful economic life such as goodwill, intellectual property or covenants-not-to-compete. For tangible assets with a limited life (raw land is usually exempt because it has unlimited life) the term used for this concept is *depreciation* and for wasting assets (natural resources) it is *depletion*. Prior to FAS 142, purchased goodwill was amortized for financial accounting purposes over no longer than 40 years, and that amortization decreased the reported earnings of the surviving enterprise. For each year after an acquisition, acquirer had to charge at least 1/40th of the goodwill account created by the acquisition against its earnings, reducing reported net profits. (In *pooling accounting*, discussed in subsection B below, an acquisition did not create a new goodwill value on the balance sheet of the surviving enterprise. The old rules on the amortization of purchased goodwill, therefore, often made the pooling accounting alternative more attractive to acquirer.) Under FAS 142, the mandatory amortization of goodwill over no longer than 40 years has been supplanted by a write-down of goodwill only in the event of a demonstrated impairment of its fair value, so the immediate impact on earnings is postponed. The new amortization rules apply to all combinations completed after June 30, 2001, and the new rules must be used even for "old" deals in financial statements for fiscal years beginning after December 15, 2001.

Goodwill is to be tested for impairment of its fair value at least annually, but certain events may require an earlier test. Goodwill should be tested for impairment between annual tests in instances such as an event or circumstance that would more likely than not reduce the fair value of a reporting unit below its carrying amount and it is unlikely that the situation would reverse before the next annual test (e.g., a significant adverse change in the business climate or market, a legal issue, an action by regulators, unanticipated competition, or a loss of key personnel) or a more-likely-than-not expectation that a reporting unit (or a significant portion of a reporting unit) will be sold or otherwise disposed of.

The cost of an acquired intangible asset recognized separately from goodwill is amortized over the asset's useful economic life. Furthermore, FAS 142 does not change the requirement of FAS 2, "Accounting for Research and Development Costs," that costs assigned to assets to be used in a particular research and development project and that have "no alternative future uses," in research and development projects or otherwise, shall be charged to expense at the date of consummation of the combination. A portion of the purchase price could therefore be allocated to such costs and written off by the surviving enterprise in one year (see FASB Interpretation No. 4, ¶ 5).

B. Pooling Accounting: A Historical Account

APB Opinion 16, "Business Combinations," from the time of its release in 1970 until its rescission by FAS 141, generally permitted two methods of accounting—the *purchase method* described above and the *pooling method*. The parties to the transaction could, as a practical matter, elect purchase or pooling treatment through the manner in which the transaction was structured. If pooling was not available, purchase accounting was the default method of accounting.

The pooling method was controversial, but some representatives of industry argued that mandatory purchase accounting, coupled with the mandatory amortization of goodwill, could so depress post-acquisition earnings that many combinations would appear financially unfeasible. Other observers countered that those arguments exaggerated the impact of an elimination of pooling because analysts often ignore the amortization of such intangibles in assessing financial reporting results. The July 2001 adoption of FAS 141 eliminated pooling accounting as a permissible alternative. However, as discussed in the preceding section, companion pronouncement FAS 142 softened the earnings impact of FAS 141 by eliminating the mandatory amortization of acquisition goodwill.

Although pooling has been eliminated as a permitted method of acquisition accounting, it was a significant chapter in the story of acquisition accounting that requires some elaboration, albeit for historical perspective. When pooling applied, the combined enterprise was treated as a merger of acquirer and target (not as an arm's-length transfer of assets at market value), and the book values of the separate enterprises carried over to the surviving entity. The consolidated financial statements were the additive combination of the financial statements of the previously separate enterprises (after intercompany eliminations and adjustments), and no goodwill was created. The absence of goodwill was not the only consequence, as the financial statements (including income statements) for prior years were restated as though the companies had always been one.

Qualifying an acquisition for pooling treatment was far from automatic, as there were 12 general criteria prescribed by APB Opinion 16 for use of the pooling method. One requirement in particular shaped the structure of many acquisitions. With very limited exceptions for fractional shares and dissenting shareholders, target common shareholders could receive only common stock in the surviving enterprise, and there could not be a pro rata distribution of cash. This requirement (as well as many of the others) reflected the premise on which pooling was based: that the surviving enterprise was a continuation of the two separate enterprises, and the target shareholders continued their undisturbed investment in the form of stock in the surviving entity. As discussed later in Chapter 8, this "solely stock" requirement also had federal income tax consequences, as it often permitted the transaction to be treated as a tax-free transaction.

§ 31. Acquisition Accounting: The Impact of the Accounting Rules on the Size of an Acquisition

The size of acquirer's stake in target will dictate the accounting treatment for the investment. Inasmuch as the equity method of accounting may apply once a 20-percent ownership threshold is achieved, acquirer might avoid that (and the share of losses of a start-up investee company) by maintaining a less than 20 percent stake. On the other hand, one might wish to hold more than 20 percent of a non-dividend paying, but profitable, company. Likewise, in the neighborhood of 50 percent ownership, acquirer must weigh the advantages of the equity method that permits only the net investment in target to be reported, and not the liabilities of target. If acquirer and target

were instead consolidated, target's debts would
appear in the consolidated statements.

CHAPTER 8

FEDERAL INCOME TAX TREATMENT OF MERGERS, ACQUISITIONS AND REORGANIZATIONS

§ 32. The "Taxable" versus "Tax-Free" (Tax-Deferred) Distinction

A. Definitions

As a practical matter most publicly-held corporations are so-called "C" corporations, the profits of which are subject to a corporate level income tax plus an income tax imposed on shareholders upon their receipt of dividends or liquidation proceeds. Reflecting the two levels of taxation, the income tax aspects of corporate reorganizations must be considered in terms of the impact on both the corporation(s) and the shareholders. In most acquisitive reorganizations there are two corporations and two sets of shareholders to consider.

As a general principle of federal income taxation, a disposition of assets (whether corporate *stock* by a target shareholder or the underlying *enterprise assets* by target itself) will generally produce the realization and immediate recognition of taxable income by the disposing party. However, the tax-free corporate reorganization provisions discussed below provide an exemption from immediate recognition of taxable gain or loss by the various parties to a corporate reorganization. See I.R.C. §§ 354, 355, 356, 361 & 368.

Viewed through an income tax lens, the structure of mergers and acquisitions is therefore often divided into *taxable* transactions, on the one hand, and *tax-free* or *tax-deferred* transactions, on the other hand. In the absence of special factors (such as a tax-exempt seller or stock purged of its built-in gain under I.R.C. § 1014 on account of the death of a shareholder), the tax-deferred label is more accurate for the latter category of transactions. A consequence of tax-free reorganization treatment is a *substituted* or *carryover* adjusted basis for stock or assets received by a party to the reorganization that preserves the built-in gain or loss in the asset, postponing the tax until a resale of the stock or assets (see § 34.E below).

B. The Choice

Considering the time value of money, if income tax consequences were the sole consideration, it would seem that the opportunity to defer income taxes into future years would channel most acquisitions into a tax-free structure. An investor could take the tax money not paid to the government and invest it, keeping the returns until such time as the tax is due. Granted, a taxable transaction produces a cost (fair market value) adjusted basis to be used by acquirer (see I.R.C. § 1012) rather than a substituted basis. However, a taxable transaction can require the payment of tax by target in the year of disposition while the income tax benefits of the cost basis may be realized by acquirer only in future years through cost recovery (i.e., depreciation or amortization) deductions and subsequent taxable dispositions of the assets.

Yet, not all transactions can fit into a tax-free structure, and some acquirers, targets and target shareholders exhibit special characteristics that diminish the benefits of a tax-free structure.

Conflicting Goals. As discussed in § 35 below, tax-free structures generally require a level of continuing proprietary (i.e., equity) investment in the reorganized enterprise. Target's shareholders may not want to take equity in the purchasing firm. As discussed later at § 34.D, even if the overall transaction is still accorded tax-free treatment, target shareholders can receive debt securities with tax-free consequences only in limited circumstances. Further, even if target's shareholders prefer an equity stake in the reorganized enterprise, acquirer might prefer to pay in cash or debt securities. For example, acquirer might desire the financial leverage, deal flexibility, lack of equity dilution, as well as the income tax deductions for the interest that debt offers.

Tax-Exempt Sellers. Due to their special tax status, some target shareholders or sellers of a business unit may not be adverse to a taxable transaction. For example, a foreign person generally can avoid U.S. income taxes on the outright sale of shares of stock in a U.S. corporation (unless the corporation holds significant U.S. real estate assets; see I.R.C. § 897). Likewise, a tax-exempt entity, such as a pension plan or charitable organization, would generally not be taxed on gains from the sale or other disposition of corporate stock held for investment (see I.R.C. § 512(b)(5)).

Target's Tax Considerations. With respect to a sale of enterprise assets, the target could have expiring net operating losses (see I.R.C. § 172) or credits that could be used to offset taxable gains. Moreover, sales of lackluster business units can produce recognized losses.

§ 33. Taxable Transactions

A. Basic Cash-for-Assets Acquisition

Under this deal structure, target sells all or a portion of its assets to acquirer for cash, notes, debt assumptions and other consideration. While stock of acquirer could be received as well, it will transform the transaction into a tax-free transaction only if acquirer's stock comprised at least a majority of the consideration received by target; this discussion will assume that is not the case.

Target will recognize gain or loss on each asset sold, based on the purchase price allocable to each asset, reduced by the asset's adjusted basis. At this time there is no reduced income tax rate for capital gains income recognized by a corporation, so any net gain on the sale could be taxed at rates as high as 35 percent. If target receives purchase money debt obligations qualifying for installment sales method reporting, target may be entitled to defer recognition of gain until payments are received (see I.R.C. §§ 453 & 453A).

The purchaser will receive a basis in each purchased asset equal to an allocable amount of the purchase price. Consequently the seller's gain or loss with respect to each asset sold, and the purchaser's basis in each asset purchased, turn upon the allocation of the purchase price among the various assets sold and purchased. As discussed in § 36.A below, I.R.C. § 1060 prescribes rules for such purchase price allocations among asset classes.

B. Basic Cash-for-Stock Acquisition

If the business unit is a subsidiary of target, the acquisition can be structured as a sale by target of the subsidiary's stock. If target itself is the focus of the acquisition and its stock is widely held, the acquisition could be structured as a cash tender offer for target's outstanding stock. A seller of stock under either scenario will recognize taxable gain or loss, computed as the difference between the selling price and the adjusted basis of the shares sold. If the sellers of stock receive purchase money debt obligations, they may be permitted to defer recognition of gains until payments are received using the installment method described in the previous section. Portions of gains from the sale by taxpayers (other than corporations) of certain stock issued after August 10, 1993 may be permanently exempted from income taxation (see generally I.R.C. § 1202) or subject to deferral if the proceeds are reinvested in similar stock (see generally I.R.C. § 1045).

While the purchaser receives an adjusted basis in the shares purchased equal to the purchase price, the adjusted basis in the underlying assets of target generally remain unchanged (assuming the absence of a "section 338 election" discussed in § 33.C below). A purchaser of stock should demand a discount in the purchase price (as compared with an acquisition of raw assets) to reflect: (1) the implicit cost of foregone cost recovery deductions that target could have claimed in the future if the adjusted basis of its assets had been increased to reflect the purchase price; and (2) the explicit cost of an income tax on the unrealized built-in gain in the assets of target that could be due upon a future disposition, in whole or in part, of those assets.

C. Some Significant Planning Choices for Stock Acquisitions

Sale of Stock of a Subsidiary With a Bootstrap Dividend. A corporation that receives dividends from other domestic (and some foreign) corporations is allowed a *dividends-received deduction* computed as 70, 80 or 100 percent of the dividend (the percentage being determined primarily by the degree of ownership in the distributing corporation; see I.R.C. § 243). A "bootstrap dividend" plan takes advantage of the dividends-received deduction through the declaration of a dividend prior to a stock sale, wagering that much of the dividend income will be eliminated by the dividends-received deduction. This planning tool involves some other technical aspects beyond the scope of this work, and the overall structure has been given a mixed reception by the courts; the timing of the dividend declaration versus the stock sale is a critical factor. See, e.g., *Waterman Steamship Corp. v. Comm'r* (5th Cir. 1970) (finding that the dividend was in substance part of the sales price and denying a dividends-received deduction); *TSN Liquidating Corp. v. United States* (5th Cir. 1980) (respecting the dividend characterization); *Litton Industries, Inc. v. Comm'r* (T.C. 1987) (respecting the dividend characterization).

Sale of Stock with an I.R.C. § 338 Election. A stock sale does not affect the adjusted basis of the assets held by target. A pure asset sale can provide the purchaser with a fair market value adjusted basis in purchased assets, but it can be cumbersome, involving numerous documents of transfer, transfer fees, third-party approvals and other complications. In response I.R.C. § 338 generally permits a *sale of stock* to be treated as a *sale of assets* for income tax purposes, although only shares of stock are changing hands. If an asset purchase is otherwise desirable, an I.R.C. § 338 election can simplify the mechanics of the acquisition while producing equivalent income tax consequences. However, the I.R.C. § 338 election does not generally offer a better income tax result than a simple stock sale because it generates an immediate tax liability that must be paid by target. While target, in the hands of acquirer, now has a purchase price adjusted basis in its assets, that result requires immediate recognition of gain or loss and payment of tax. In the absence of special circumstances (e.g., a net operating loss carryover in target, particularly one that could be of limited use after the acquisition due to the net operating loss limitation rules of I.R.C. § 382 discussed later at § 36.G or a target that is an S corporation which, unlike a C corporation, is generally subject to only one layer of taxation imposed directly on the shareholders) the purchasing corporation would usually not choose to incur the immediate tax.

If the purchasing corporation makes an I.R.C. § 338 election, target is treated for income tax purposes as if it sold all of its assets to a new corporation for the "aggregate deemed sales price" or "ADSP," and target recognizes gains or losses accordingly. Ignoring a number of complications, the ADSP can simply be the selling price of the target stock (reduced by any selling expenses of the shareholders) plus the liabilities of target. The fictional "new" corporation likewise takes a new adjusted basis in the assets corresponding to the purchase price, the "adjusted grossed-up basis" or "AGUB." In the simplest case, AGUB is computed by adding the basis of the target stock to the liabilities of the target. The allocation of the purchase price among the "purchased" assets is made under rules that also govern asset sales (see § 36.A).

There are a number of details to the I.R.C. § 338 election that must be omitted, but two of them are of fundamental importance in structuring an acquisition. First, the election can be made only within a narrow time window. It may be made not later than the 15th day of the ninth month, beginning after the month in which the *acquisition date* occurs (see I.R.C. § 338(g)). The acquisition date is the first day on which there is a *qualified stock purchase* (see I.R.C. § 338(h)(2)). Second, the election window opens only if there is a qualified stock purchase, which is limited to any transaction or series of transactions in which stock that is at least 80 percent of the voting power of the corporation and at least 80 percent of the total value of the stock of the corporation is acquired, *by purchase* (this excludes, among other transactions, tax-free stock exchanges), *during the 12-month acquisition period* (see I.R.C. § 338(d)(3)). If the purchasing corporation acquired a greater than 20-percent position in target at some time in the past in a *toehold* or *creeping* acquisition, but subsequently acquires the balance of the shares in one or more transactions within a 12-month period, I.R.C. § 338 may not apply because an 80 percent position was not purchased within the 12-month period.

Sale of Stock with I.R.C. §338(h)(10) Election. In the I.R.C. § 338 election discussed above, two layers of tax are imposed. First, target computes gain or loss on the sale of its assets through the deemed sale produced by the I.R.C. § 338 election. Second, the seller of the shares computes gain or loss on the shares sold by subtracting the adjusted basis of the shares from the sales price. Although I.R.C. § 338 may offer little advantage under the current corporate income tax provisions, I.R.C. § 338(h)(10) has continued vitality.

The I.R.C. § 338(h)(10) election is made jointly by the seller and purchaser, and can be made only if target is part of an affiliated group of corporations (generally speaking, it must be at least an 80-percent-owned subsidiary of another corporation) or is an S corporation (the special treatment of S corporations and shareholders is otherwise beyond the scope of this work).

If the I.R.C. § 338(h)(10) election is made, two results follow. First, target can be included as a member of a consolidated group that includes the selling corporation, so that the gains and losses from the deemed asset sale could be combined with other losses, income or credits of the consolidated group. See I.R.C. §§ 338(h)(9), (h)(10)(A). Second, no gain or loss is recognized on the sale of the stock of target. In many cases, the only gain or loss recognized is that produced by the deemed asset sale, so only one layer of tax is imposed.

In weighing the desirability of an I.R.C. § 338(h)(10) election to a C corporation seller, one generally would compare the taxable gain produced by a sale of target stock (without an I.R.C. § 338 election) with the taxable gain produced by a sale of target's assets (the practical tax result of the I.R.C. § 338(h)(10) election). However, since the target stock (without an I.R.C. § 338 election) and target's assets with a fair market value tax basis have different after-tax values to the purchaser, those potential price differences also must be considered in the calculation.

Liquidating the Target: The I.R.C. § 332 Alternative. The I.R.C. § 338(h)(10) election permits the sale of a subsidiary's stock to be treated as a sale of assets, but without the need for conveyancing and transfer documents for the assets "transferred." If the seller is not troubled by the need for conveyancing and transfer documents, and indeed, if the purchaser insists on receiving a transfer of assets, rather than accepting stock in the subsidiary, a similar income tax result can be achieved by first liquidating the subsidiary into the parent corporation and then selling the assets to the purchaser (or selling the assets to the purchaser and then liquidating the subsidiary with a distribution of the cash proceeds). The liquidation of an 80-percent-controlled subsidiary is generally not a taxable event to either the subsidiary or the parent corporation. See I.R.C. §§ 332 & 337. The parent corporation receives the subsidiary's basis in each of the assets received (see I.R.C. § 334(b)); the parent corporation's basis in the subsidiary's stock is irrelevant. As with an I.R.C. § 338(h)(10) election, the parent corporation's gain or loss on the sale of the assets will be determined with reference to the subsidiary's adjusted basis in the assets. Since the parent need not sell all of the assets to the purchasing party, this approach may be preferable to an I.R.C. § 338(h)(10) election if target holds assets that acquirer does not want.

D. Cash-Out Mergers

A sale of all of target's assets, and the elimination of target as a corporation, may be accomplished through a cash-out forward merger, in which target is merged into the purchasing corporation, and target's shareholders receive cash and/or debt in exchange for their stock in target. Although considered a merger for state law purposes, the IRS may view the transaction as a taxable sale of the assets of target, followed by a liquidation of target, for which target's shareholders will recognize gain or loss as if they sold their shares (see I.R.C. § 331; Rev. Rul. 69-6, 1969-1 C.B. 104). If target's shareholders receive debt obligations of the purchasing corporation, installment sales reporting of the gain may be available. See I.R.C. § 453(h).

Likewise, the equivalent of a taxable sale of stock can be achieved through a cash-out reverse subsidiary merger, a triangular merger (see Diagram 9 in Chapter One) in which the purchasing corporation forms a subsidiary that merges into target, with the target surviving and with target's shareholders receiving cash and/or debt in exchange for their stock in target. If the purchasing corporation's cash or debt obligations are used to buy out target's shareholders, the transaction may be treated for income tax purposes as a purchase of the target shareholders' stock. See, e.g., Rev. Rul. 73-427, 1973-2 C.B. 301.

§ 34. Tax-Free Transactions: An Overview

A. I.R.C. § 368: The Base Definitions

The most well-known Internal Revenue Code section governing this area is I.R.C. § 368, and while it is only definitional, those definitions unlock the related nonrecognition provisions found elsewhere. There are seven principal reorganization categories defined in I.R.C. § 368(a)(1)(A)-(G), and the income tax paragraph designations are used to identify the transactions in common usage.

For example, it is quite common to hear or read about a "B reorg" without elaboration, referring to I.R.C. § 368(a)(1)(B) discussed below.

Once the term "reorganization" is defined, the statute further defines who is "a party to a reorganization," which is a phrase used throughout the companion nonrecognition provisions. The transactions must also proceed pursuant to a "plan of reorganization." See Treas. Reg. § 1.368-1(c).

B. I.R.C. § 1032: Nonrecognition for Acquiring Corporation

Acquirer will usually issue shares or use treasury stock in exchange for assets of target. The issuance or transfer of shares for this purpose is not a taxable event (see I.R.C. § 1032).

C. I.R.C. § 361: Nonrecognition for Target Corporation

The target will often exchange its property solely for stock or securities of the acquiring corporation. This is not a taxable event (see I.R.C. § 361(a)). Even if target receives other property, such as cash, it still will not be a taxable event to target if it distributes all of the property pursuant to the plan of reorganization (see I.R.C. § 361(b)). Although there are potential complications, generally speaking I.R.C. § 361 immunizes target from recognition of gain or loss on the transfer of its assets to the acquiring corporation in exchange for stock, securities or cash, which are in turn distributed to target's shareholders pursuant to the plan of reorganization.

D. I.R.C. §§ 354 & 356: Nonrecognition for Shareholders and Bondholders

No gain or loss shall be recognized if stock or securities in a corporation that is a party to a reorganization is exchanged solely for stock or securities in such corporation (for example, in a recapitalization of a single corporation) or in another corporation a party to the reorganization (for example, in an acquisitive merger). See I.R.C. § 354(a)(1). If the shareholder receives cash or other property gain may be recognized, but in an amount not to exceed the sum of such money and the fair market value of the other property received. The gain may be treated as capital gain or as a dividend, depending upon whether the exchange "has the effect of the distribution of a dividend." See I.R.C. § 356(a); *Clark v. Comm'r* (U.S. 1989); Rev. Rul. 93-61, 1993-2 C.B. 118.

Stock exchanged for stock is a simple matter that will almost always be a nonrecognition transaction if the other reorganization requirements are met. However, if securities (i.e., debt) are received and no such securities are surrendered, the fair market value of the securities will be treated like the receipt of cash, triggering income to the recipient. Even if securities are surrendered, but the principal amount of the securities received exceeds the principal amount of the securities surrendered, the fair market value of such excess is likewise treated like the receipt of cash (see I.R.C. § 356(d)).

Because the receipt of stock usually enjoys nonrecognition treatment while the receipt of securities may trigger gain, preferred stock offers a compromise. The Taxpayer Relief Act of 1997 responded to the potential abuses by treating most "nonqualified preferred stock" as the equivalent of cash, so its receipt will produce income to the distributee. Nonqualified preferred stock generally means preferred stock having functionally debt-like features such as: shareholder put rights; mandatory redemption provisions; corporation call rights if, as of the issue date, it is more likely than not that such right will be exercised; or a dividend rate varying with reference to interest rates, commodity prices, or similar indices.

E. I.R.C. §§ 362 & 358: Adjusted Basis Rules

To preserve the gain or loss otherwise deferred by I.R.C. § 361, the transferee corporation's basis in the property acquired is the same as it would be in the hands of the transferor, increased by any gain recognized by the transferor on such transfer. Likewise, a shareholder's basis in stock or securities received in a reorganization is the basis of the property exchanged decreased by the fair market value of any other property or money received by the taxpayer and increased by the amount of income recognized in the transaction (see I.R.C. § 358(a)).

§ 35. The Reorganization Categories of I.R.C. § 368

A. "A" Reorganizations

This is the most widely-used structure. Before some complications discussed below, the "A" merger is described simply as "a statutory merger or consolidation." See I.R.C. § 368(a)(1)(A). The regulations further state that the merger or consolidation must be "effected pursuant to the corporation laws of the United States or a State or Territory or the District of Columbia." See Treas. Reg. § 1.368-2(b)(1).

Even if the state merger law would refer to a reorganization as a "merger," it still may not be respected for federal tax purposes. The IRS, for example, has ruled that to qualify as an A merger, the reorganization must end target's existence and must result in a single acquiring corporation acquiring target's assets. See Rev. Rul. 2000-5, 2000-5 I.R.B. 436; Prop. Treas. Reg. § 1.368-2(b)(1).

Continuity of Proprietary Interest. Although not expressly required by the statute (but practically required by the structure of some of the reorganizations, such as the B reorganization), courts and the IRS require "continuity of proprietary interest" in the acquiring corporation by target's shareholders. See Treas. Reg. § 1.368-1(e)(1). This reflects the premise that the tax-free reorganization provisions represent only a change in the form of ownership, and not a "cashing out," and target's shareholders are reinvesting in the reorganized corporation. For ruling purposes the IRS requires that at least 50 percent of the consideration to be received by target's shareholders in the aggregate be stock of the acquiring corporation. See Rev. Proc. 77-37, 1977-2 C.B. 568. An early Supreme Court decision recognized a transaction in which only 38 percent of the consideration was in the form of stock (see *John A. Nelson Co. v. Helvering* (U.S. 1935)), but publicly-traded companies are often reluctant to proceed without a favorable IRS ruling.

Even if the overall reorganization qualifies for tax-free status, shareholders will usually be required to recognize income to the extent of other non-qualifying consideration received. See I.R.C. § 356, discussed at § 34.D.

In 1998 the IRS issued regulations (amended in 2000) that deal with the proprietary interest requirement in a liberal manner, stating as a general proposition that

> a mere disposition of stock of the target corporation prior to a potential reorganization to persons not related...to the target corporation or to persons not related...[to] the issuing corporation is disregarded and a mere disposi-

tion of stock of the issuing corporation received in a potential reorganization to persons not related...to the issuing corporation is disregarded.

Treas. Reg. § 1.368-1(e)(1)(i). If corporate parties related to the target or to the issuing (acquiring) corporation are involved in such sales or redemptions, the dispositions may destroy continuity of proprietary interest. Subject to those limitations, target shareholders can generally dispose of their stock prior to or following the reorganization without jeopardizing the overall tax-free reorganization treatment for those shareholders who wish to retain equity stakes. Despite the general prohibition on payments that are traceable, directly or indirectly, to the acquiring corporation, the IRS approved post-reorganization *open market* stock repurchases by an acquiring corporation, pursuant to a plan in place before the reorganization but which was amended to increase the number of repurchased shares to address the dilution from the issuance of the additional shares required for the reorganization. See Rev. Rul. 99-58, 1999-2 C.B. 701.

Continuity of Business Enterprise. The IRS requires "continuity of business enterprise," meaning that the acquiring corporation either continue target's historic business or use a significant portion of target's historic business assets in a business. See Treas. Reg. § 1.368-1(d)(1).

Forward Triangular Merger. This is the most common form of tax-free reorganization for publicly-traded companies. In a forward triangular merger, an acquiring corporation creates a subsidiary and target merges into the subsidiary (with target disappearing), and the target shareholders receive at least 50 percent of the acquisition consideration in the form of stock of the parent corporation (the balance can be cash, debt securities or other property). This is a tax-free acquisition so long as: (1) the parent corporation controls the subsidiary; (2) stock of the parent corporation is used and no stock of the subsidiary is used; (3) the transaction would otherwise have qualified as an A merger had the merger been into the parent corporation (i.e., the transaction is under a State or Territory merger law, and continuity of proprietary interest—hence the 50 percent requirement noted above—and business enterprise is satisfied); and (4) substantially all of the properties of target are acquired.

As compared with a direct merger of the parent acquiring corporation and target, the fourth requirement is about the only additional restriction (assuming the parent is not a foreign corporation, which would have precluded a direct merger). The IRS will rule that it is satisfied if "assets representing at least 90 percent of the fair market value of the net assets and at least 70 percent of the fair market value of the gross assets held by the target corporation immediately preceding the transfer" are transferred (see Rev. Proc.

77-37, 1977-2 C.B. 568). One must also respect the uncertain application of the step transaction doctrine. For example, in Revenue Ruling 72-405 (1972-2 C.B. 217) the IRS ruled that if the acquisition subsidiary is transitory by plan and subsequently liquidated into the parent corporation, the overall transaction will be viewed as a "C" reorganization discussed below, which unlike a forward "A," is more restrictive and requires the use of *voting* stock of the acquiring corporation.

Reverse Triangular Merger. The transaction is initially structured in the same manner as a forward triangular merger except that target, rather than the acquisition subsidiary, survives the merger to become a subsidiary of the acquiring corporation. This structure is not as popular because it has more restrictions; in particular cash, debt securities and other property are limited to 20 percent of the consideration for the acquisition. It would be used if the continued existence of target is necessary due to the restrictions imposed by licenses, leases, loan covenants, regulatory requirements or some other constraint.

A reverse triangular merger is tax-free so long as (1) the parent corporation controls the subsidiary which is to be eliminated in the transaction; (2) stock of the parent corporation is used as consideration for the merger; (3) the corporation surviving the merger holds substantially all of its properties and the properties of the merged corporation (other than the stock of the parent corporation); and (4) in the transaction former shareholders of the surviving target exchange, for an amount of voting stock of the parent corporation, an amount of stock in the surviving corporation which constitutes control of target. Not only must the reorganization meet the "substantially all properties" test, but the fourth requirement mandates that the target shareholders receive *voting* stock in the parent corporation *and* that in the aggregate the target shareholders must relinquish, in exchange for such voting stock, stock which represents control (i.e., 80 percent) of the surviving target.

B. "B" Reorganizations

This reorganization is the acquisition by one corporation, in exchange solely for all or part of its voting stock, of stock of another corporation if, immediately after the acquisition, the acquiring corporation has control (generally at least 80 percent ownership as defined in I.R.C. § 368(c)) of such other corporation. The statute permits a triangular acquisition where a subsidiary controlled by the acquiring corporation could use stock of the parent corporation in the exchange.

This structure is very restrictive because the acquiring corporation must use *voting* stock and must use *solely* voting stock. While there are some administrative exceptions for the payment of some of target's expenses of the transaction, such as legal and accounting fees (see Rev. Rul. 73-54,

1973-1 C.B. 187) and for the cash redemption of fractional shares (see Rev. Rul. 66-365, 1966-2 C.B. 116), the voting stock requirement is otherwise strictly applied; the reorganization is disqualified if target's shareholders receive any cash, debt securities (except for exchanges or purchases of debt securities apart from, and not constituting indirect additional consideration for, the stock acquisition; see Rev. Rul. 98-10, 1998-1 C.B. 643), nonvoting stock or other property. Early toehold acquisitions for cash, followed by a later acquisition of control solely for stock are risky unless the taxpayer can demonstrate that the toehold acquisition was unrelated to the subsequent acquisition of control for stock. That proof will be very factual, and public corporations may be reluctant to risk a "creeping" B reorganization with cash consideration for any of the acquisitions. See, e.g., *Chapman v. Comm'r* (1st Cir. 1980) (holding that "solely for stock" applies to all acquisitions of stock pursuant to the plan, even if the 80 percent control stake in target were solely for stock, but not reaching the issue of whether the toehold was a severable transaction).

The acquiring corporation's assumption of target obligations personally guaranteed by target shareholders must be approached with care to avoid treatment as disqualifying boot, particularly if target is inadequately capitalized. Compare Rev. Rul. 79-4, 1979-1 C.B. 150 (assumption treated as consideration for target stock); Rev. Rul. 79-89, 1979-1 C.B. 152 (contribution of cash by acquiring corporation to discharge debt obligations of target not treated as consideration for target stock).

C. "C" Reorganizations

A "C" reorganization is the acquisition by one corporation, in exchange solely for all or a part of its voting stock, of substantially all of the properties of another corporation (see I.R.C. § 368(a)(1)(C)). Triangular structures are permitted which allow a subsidiary to acquire target's assets in exchange solely for voting stock of a parent corporation. Id. Alternatively, the parent corporation can acquire the assets of target and drop part or all of them into a subsidiary (see I.R.C. § 368(a)(2)(C)). Unless a waiver is granted by the IRS, target must distribute to its shareholders all the stock, securities and other properties it receives, as well as its other properties, pursuant to the plan of reorganization, and liquidate (see I.R.C. § 368(a)(2)(G)).

This reorganization is often referred to as a "practical merger" because the result resembles a merger of target into the acquirer. However, it is much more restrictive. First, voting stock of the acquiring corporation must be used. Second, substantially all of the properties of target must be acquired. Third, under the so-called "boot relaxation rule," consideration besides voting stock can be used in limited amounts. Target liabilities that the acquirer assumes or takes the assets subject to are ignored if no consideration other than voting stock is used (see I.R.C. § 368(a)(1)(C)). However, if even $1 of other consideration is utilized, voting stock must be exchanged for assets of target, the fair market value of which is at least 80 percent of the fair market value of all of the property of target and debts assumed or taken subject to are treated as money paid for the property. Even a modest level of debt can exceed the 20 percent limit. The money or other property to which the 20 percent rule is applied can include money or other property paid to acquire toehold positions in target unless the stock was, for example, "purchased several years ago in an unrelated transaction" (see Treas. Reg. § 1.368-2(d)(4)).

Single Firm Reorganizations. The A, B and C reorganizations above are *acquisitive* in nature. Those that follow primarily deal with reorganizations of a single corporation.

D. "D" Reorganizations

A "D" reorganization is described as a transfer by a corporation of all or part of its assets to another corporation if, immediately after the transfer, the transferor, one or more of its shareholders, or any combination thereof, is in control of the corporation to which the assets are transferred, but only if, pursuant to the plan, stock or securities of the transferee corporation are distributed in a transaction that qualifies under I.R.C. §§ 354, 355 or 356 (see I.R.C. § 368(a)(1)(D)). The required distribution avenues create two principal types of

D reorganizations, governed by I.R.C. §§ 354 or 355, since I.R.C. § 356 adds nothing if no disqualified debt, money or property is involved.

I.R.C. § 354 states that its exemption from taxation shall not apply to distributions of stock or securities in a D reorganization unless the corporation to which the assets are transferred acquires substantially all of the assets of the transferor (applying the 90/70 test discussed earlier in connection with forward triangular mergers), and the stock, securities and other properties received by such transferor, as well as the other properties of such transferor, are distributed in pursuance of the plan of reorganization. See I.R.C. § 354(b). This type of D reorganization operates as a wholesale reincorporation of the old corporation into a new corporation and is not important to mergers and acquisitions of public companies.

The other type of D reorganization involves the creation of a subsidiary that is in turn distributed to shareholders in a *divisive reorganization.* Divisive reorganizations are governed by I.R.C. § 355, which permits a single corporation to be split, free of immediate tax, into multiple corporations. If I.R.C. § 355 applies, neither the distributing corporation nor the distributee shareholder recognizes income upon the distribution of the stock of a subsidiary. Very generally speaking, this tax-free treatment is available if (1) the distributing corporation distributes to a shareholder with respect to its stock, stock of a corporation (the subsidiary) that it controls immediately before the distribution; (2) the transaction was not used principally as a device for the distribution of earnings and profits of the distributing corporation or the controlled corporation (this disguised dividend test is usually the most difficult part of the statute to satisfy for closely-held corporations, but if the distributing corporation is publicly traded and widely held, with a no-greater-than-5 percent shareholder, that is nondevice evidence under Treas. Reg. § 1.355-2(d)(3)(iii)); (3) the distributing corporation and the controlled corporation are engaged immediately after the distribution in the active conduct of a trade or business that has been actively conducted throughout the previous five-year period (this may be difficult for emerging companies); (4) the distributing corporation distributes all of the stock of the controlled corporation held by it; and (5) there is a business purpose for the transaction.

The most common divisive reorganization for public corporations is the *spin-off*. In a spin-off, the corporation places the assets of a business unit (such as a division) in a newly-formed subsidiary using a D reorganization. If the business unit is already in a subsidiary then the preparatory D reorganization is unnecessary. The corporation then distributes stock of the subsidiary to its shareholders pro rata in a manner that resembles a dividend for state law purposes. At the conclusion of the transaction, the same shareholders own shares of the original corporation plus shares of the new corporation, and both companies may now be publicly traded as separate stocks, hopefully enhancing the aggregate market value of the two stocks. If I.R.C. § 355 applies, the transaction is tax-free as to the distributing corporation as well as the distributee shareholders. Most public companies will request a private ruling from the IRS confirming that the transaction is tax-free. The Taxpayer Relief Act of 1997 placed complex new limitations on the use of so-called "Morris Trust" transactions (*Commissioner v. Morris Trust* (4th Cir. 1966)), in which spin-off transactions are generally used prior to a merger to dispose of target assets that are not desired by the acquiring merger party (see I.R.C. § 355(e)).

There are two other divisive structures. In the *split-off* transaction, the stock of the subsidiary is not distributed pro rata, but is instead distributed only to some of the distributing corporation's shareholders in complete redemption of their stock. At the conclusion of the transaction, one group of shareholders owns the distributing corporation, and another group of shareholders owns the distributed corporation. This technique is often employed to split corporate assets, on a tax-free basis, among feuding shareholders in a closely-held corporation. The *split-up* transaction involves the creation of multiple subsidiaries, the stock of which is distributed to all of the shareholders in liquidation of the original corporation, which ceases to exist. A regulator, for example, might require the split-up of a public corporation.

E. "E" Reorganizations

This reorganization deals only with a single corporation and is defined in the Internal Revenue Code simply as "a recapitalization." See I.R.C. § 368(a)(1)(E). It is very flexible, and the regulations permit the issuance of preferred shares to bondholders, the surrender of preferred stock for no par value common stock, the issuance of preferred stock for outstanding common stock, and the exchange of preferred stock with various priorities for a new issue of common stock having no such rights. See Treas. Reg. § 1.368-2(e). One can encounter transactions of this nature in reorganizing the capital structure of a corporation for an initial public offering. Bonds may also be exchanged for bonds, mindful of the rule that if the principal amount of the bonds received exceeds that of the bonds surrendered, the fair market value of the excess will produce taxable gain. See I.R.C. § 356 (discussed earlier at § 34.D). Furthermore, with the issuance of stock to bondholders or bonds for bonds, the corporation must consider the cancellation of indebtedness income consequences (see I.R.C. § 108(e)(10)).

Bonds received for stock are troublesome, because it is likely that this transaction will be treated as a taxable redemption of the stock. See *Bazley v. Comm'r* (U.S. 1947); I.R.C. § 356.

F. "F" Reorganizations

An "F" reorganization is "a mere change in identity, form, or place of organization of one corporation, however effected." See I.R.C. § 368(a)(1)(F). While extending to mundane transactions such as corporate name changes, this provision is also helpful in changing the place of incorporation. For example, a Nevada corporation can be merged into a newly-formed Delaware shell as an F reorganization. While that would also qualify as an A reorganization, F reorganization status can avoid certain limitations on the use of corporate attributes, such as net operating losses.

G. "G" Reorganizations

"G" reorganizations deal with insolvency reorganizations.

§ 36. Collateral Income Tax Provisions Impacting Merger and Acquisition Transactions

While the taxable versus tax-free distinction is the principal income tax consideration in deal structure, other income tax provisions (such as the amortization of goodwill and limits on interest expense deductibility) also play planning roles. Some of the provisions are relevant only to taxable transactions, and vice versa. Others impact both groups of transactions.

A. Purchase Price Allocations

Special income tax considerations apply to the transfer of a group of assets that constitute a trade or business in the hands of either the seller or the purchaser (a so-called "applicable asset acquisition"). First, the seller and purchaser can agree in writing as to the allocation of the consideration or fair market value of any assets, and it will be binding on both parties unless the IRS determines that the parties' allocations are not appropriate (see I.R.C. § 1060(a)). Second, the seller and the purchaser are each required to furnish information about the transaction, particularly the allocation of the purchase price among the assets transferred, to the IRS (see I.R.C. § 1060(b)). Third, IRS regulations prescribe a method of allocating the purchase price among the assets transferred. Those regulations are found under I.R.C. § 338, but the allocation methods apply to outright asset sales as well as deemed asset sales under I.R.C. § 338.

The allocation regulations designate seven classes of assets. Class I assets are highly liquid cash, demand deposits and similar items. Class II assets include certificates of deposit, U.S. government securities, foreign currency and readily marketable stock or securities. Class III assets include accounts receivable, mortgages and credit card receivables from customers arising in the ordinary course of business. Class IV assets are inventories. Class V assets are assets not in any other class. Class VI assets are I.R.C. § 197 intan-

gibles (discussed below) other than goodwill and
going concern value. Class VII assets are goodwill
and going concern value.

The regulations first reduce the purchase price
by the Class I assets transferred by the seller. The
remaining consideration is allocated among the
Class II assets and so on, such that Class VII
becomes a residual category. As discussed in the
following section, goodwill purchased after 1993
can be amortized over 15 years, and that has
reduced the negative income tax consequences of
allocating residual value to that category.

Section 197 Intangibles. The Revenue
Reconciliation Act of 1993 dramatically changed
the income tax treatment of acquired intangible
assets with the adoption of a new I.R.C. § 197.
I.R.C. § 197 permits amortization of a "section 197
intangible" over a 15-year period beginning with
the month in which the intangible was acquired.
I.R.C. § 197 specifically includes as a section 197
intangible a broad list of property interests,
including goodwill, going concern value, workforce
in place, business books and records, operating
systems, customer lists, patents, copyrights,
formulae, processes, designs, patterns, know-how,
licenses or permits, covenants not to compete,
franchises, trademarks, trade names, customer-
based intangibles, supplier-based intangibles, and
the deposit base of a financial institution.
Purchased goodwill had not previously been
amortizable, although taxpayers had some success

in claiming amortization deductions by separating other identifiable assets with limited lives from business goodwill. Covenants not to compete, which under prior law could be amortized over the term of the agreement, were made less attractive if the term is less than the 15-year statutory period.

B. Greenmail Payments

Some corporations took the position that payments to redeem the stock of a corporate "raider" were currently deductible as a business expense. I.R.C. § 162(k) now broadly denies a deduction for any amount paid or incurred by a corporation in connection with the reacquisition of its stock or the stock of certain related persons. Some related expenditures, such as interest expense and loan costs, are still deductible.

I.R.C. § 5881 in turn imposes an excise tax of 50 percent of gain or other income on the recipient of greenmail. "Greenmail" means any consideration transferred by a corporation (or any person acting in concert with such corporation) to directly or indirectly acquire stock of such corporation from any shareholder if such shareholder held such stock for less than two years before entering into the agreement to make the transfer. At some time during the two-year period ending on the date of such acquisition such shareholder (or any person acting in concert with such shareholder or any related persons) must have made or threatened to make a public tender offer for stock of such corporation. The acquisition also must be pursuant to an offer that was not made on the same terms to all shareholders.

C. I.R.C. § 279 Debt

The Tax Reform Act of 1969 added I.R.C. § 279 with the aim of curbing the deductibility of interest on debt used for corporate acquisitions. The provision limits a corporation's interest deduction on account of "corporate acquisition indebtedness" to a maximum of $5 million. The provision generally applies only if the debt is: (1) subordinated to the claims of trade creditors or any substantial amount of unsecured indebtedness of the corporation; and (2) convertible into stock of the issuing corporation. Furthermore, as of the last day of the taxable year of the year of issue, the debt-to-equity ratio of the issuing corporation must exceed 2:1 or the projected earnings must not exceed three times the annual interest to be paid or incurred. The use of "straight" debt that is not convertible into the issuer's stock has reportedly rendered I.R.C. § 279 inapplicable to many transactions.

D. Junk Bonds: High-Yield Discount Obligations

The Omnibus Budget Reconciliation Act of 1989 introduced another limit on the use of high-yield ("junk") bonds in corporate acquisitions where the payment of interest is significantly postponed into later years. In the case of an "applicable high-yield discount obligation" issued by a corporation, no deduction is ever allowed for the "disqualified portion" of the original issue discount on the obligation, and the remainder of the original issue discount is not deductible until paid. See I.R.C. § 163(e)(5). An "applicable high-yield discount obligation" is a debt instrument with a term of more than five years, a yield to maturity that exceeds the applicable federal rate in effect under I.R.C. § 1274(d) (tied to government securities) for the calendar month of issuance plus five percentage points, and the instrument has "significant" original issue discount. Original issue discount is significant if the amount of original issue discount that would be accrued in the first five years of the instrument exceeds the sum of the aggregate amount of interest to be paid during such period plus the product of the issue price of the instrument and its yield to maturity.

The disqualified portion of the original issue discount is the lesser of the original issue discount or the total return on such obligation multiplied by a fraction, the numerator of which is the "disqualified yield" and the denominator of which is the yield to maturity. The disqualified yield is the yield to maturity in excess of the applicable federal rate in effect under I.R.C. § 1274(d) for the calendar month of issuance plus six percentage points.

E. Net Operating Loss Carry-Back Limitations: CERT

I.R.C. § 172 permits a corporation that has experienced net operating losses to carry those losses back to two prior years (and obtain a tax refund if those years were profitable), and then forward 20 years (see I.R.C. § 172(b)). A corporation incurring large amounts of interest expense in connection with an acquisition, or simply to leverage assets to produce cash for dividends and stock repurchases, could create a net operating loss that could be carried back to prior years, securing tax refunds for those years. The Omnibus Budget Reconciliation Act of 1989 introduced a narrow provision aimed at limiting the use of debt in these situations. It applies only if the interest deductions are of a magnitude that creates net operating losses.

The amount of a net operating loss of a corporation is reduced by a portion of the interest deductions attributable to a "corporate equity reduction transaction," known as a "CERT." See I.R.C. § 172(h). A CERT includes the acquisition by a corporation of stock in another corporation representing 50 percent or more (by vote or value) of the stock in the target. The statute does not apply to asset purchases or to stock purchases for which an I.R.C. § 338 election is made or to purchases of stock of corporations that are already affiliated with the purchaser. A CERT also includes an excess distribution, defined as aggregate distributions (including redemptions) made during a taxable year by a corporation with respect to its stock in excess of the greater of 150 percent of the average of such distributions over the three immediately preceding taxable years or 10 percent of the fair market value of the stock of such corporation as of the beginning of the year. This provision could apply to a leveraged going-private transaction.

F. Limitations on a Purchasing Firm's Use of Target's Net Operating Loss Carry-Forwards

As noted above, a net operating loss can be carried forward 20 years from the taxable year in which it arose. If target owns that loss, the potential shelter from taxation can be valuable to target if its fortunes improve or to an acquiring corporation that might be entitled to offset such losses against its profits (subject to consolidated income tax return considerations).

Section 382. I.R.C. § 382 limits the utilization of a net operating loss for the periods following an acquisition, and companion I.R.C. § 383 places limitations on the utilization of certain tax credits. Such limits apply irrespective of whether the acquisition takes the form of a taxable or a tax-free acquisition (except that if an I.R.C. § 338 election is made, the net operating losses are extinguished for future use).

Speaking very generally, there is a triggering ownership change if the percentage of stock of the loss corporation owned by one or more 5 percent shareholders has increased by more than 50 percentage points (not simply 50 percent) over the lowest percentage of stock of the loss corporation owned by such shareholders at any time during a "testing period" which, subject to exceptions, generally looks back three years. See I.R.C. § 382(g). In publicly-traded corporations, preacquisition minority target shareholders may be treated as a single 5 percent shareholder for this purpose.

Subject to various exceptions, if the successor corporation does not continue the business enterprise of target at all times during the two-year period beginning on the date when the 50-percentage-point change of ownership occurred, none of the net operating loss may be used in post-change years. Even if the business enterprise is continued, the "section 382 limitation" for any post-change year is, subject to exceptions, limited to the product of the value of target immediately before the ownership change multiplied by the "long-term tax-exempt rate" (a rate tied to long-term government securities, adjusted for differences between taxable and tax-exempt obligations). The amount of the I.R.C. § 382 limitation is fixed at the time of the acquisition. The use of the tax benefits from the net operating loss in excess of the annual § 382 limitation is consequently deferred into future years and therefore has less present value. Moreover, at some point the overall carryover limitation of a maximum of 20 years prescribed by I.R.C. § 172 will apply, denying the further use of any remaining losses.

Reverse Acquisitions. Rather than it being acquired, target might consider the acquisition of another corporation (or the assets of such a corporation in a tax-deferred A, C or D reorganization) that holds appreciated assets, so that the gain from a post-acquisition disposition of those assets could be absorbed by the operating loss carry-forwards. I.R.C. § 382 could apply to this transaction if the relative values of the acquiring and acquired corporations are such that the shareholders of the acquired corporation hold more than 50 percent of the surviving post-acquisition entity. Even if I.R.C. § 382 does not apply, I.R.C. § 384 would deny application of the preacquisition net operating loss carry-forwards of the acquiring corporation to built-in gains of the acquired corporation recognized within five years after the acquisition. I.R.C. § 384 has a number of exceptions and qualifications.

Section 269. Acquisition of a corporation, the principal purpose of which is evasion or avoidance of federal income taxes, may also run afoul of the broad sweep of I.R.C. § 269, with possible disallowance of the claimed deduction or credit. While this section is a noted acquisition risk factor in dealing with a target that possesses losses or credits, I.R.C. §§ 382, 383 and 384 are more certain in application and often a greater concern for acquirers.

G. Golden Parachute Payments

I.R.C. § 280G denies a deduction "for any excess parachute payment." See I.R.C. § 280G(a). An "excess" parachute payment is an amount equal to the excess of a parachute payment over a base amount allocated to such payment. A "parachute payment" includes any compensation to or for the benefit of employees, independent contractors, officers, shareholders or highly-compensated individuals if the payment is contingent on a change in the ownership or effective control of the corporation or in the ownership of a substantial portion of the assets of the corporation, and the aggregate present value (determined using the government securities applicable federal rate of I.R.C. § 1274) of the payments equals or exceeds an amount equal to three times the base amount. The "base amount" is the annualized compensation which was includable in the gross income of the individual for the most recent five taxable years ending before the date on which the change in ownership or control occurs (or such portion of such period during which the individual performed personal services for the corporation). Exceptions apply if a taxpayer establishes by clear and convincing evidence that the compensation is reasonable for personal services actually rendered or to be rendered, before or on or after the date of the change of control or ownership.

H. Deductibility of Acquisition Expenses

The costs of an acquisition (e.g., fees to attorneys, accountants and underwriters) can be substantial. As to the acquiring corporation, the costs of obtaining debt financing can be amortized over the term of the applicable obligations. See Rev. Rul. 70-359, 1970-2 C.B. 103. The expenses of obtaining equity financing, however, are neither deductible nor amortizable and are therefore more costly from an income tax perspective. See Rev. Rul. 69-330, 1969-1 C.B. 51. However, maintenance costs such as registrar and transfer agent fees (Rev. Rul. 69-615, 1969-2 C.B. 26) and SEC reporting (Rev. Rul. 65-13, 1965-1 C.B. 87) are generally deductible currently. The costs of acquiring specific target assets will usually be added to the basis of the acquired property and can be amortized or depreciated if that is otherwise allowed for the acquired asset.

With respect to target, there is greater uncertainty. The Supreme Court has held that the costs of a friendly takeover are capitalized and not immediately deductible if there are future benefits from the transaction, even if not a separate or distinct asset. See *INDOPCO, Inc. v. Comm'r* (U.S. 1992). Amortization of those costs may not be allowed if a specific asset with a definite useful economic life cannot be identified. The facts of *INDOPCO* dealt with a friendly takeover. In the view of the Tax Court, the costs of a hostile takeover are capitalized if the target succumbs to the

acquisition and it offers future benefits. See, e.g.,
A.E. Staley Manufacturing Co. v. Comm'r (T.C.
1995). However, the Seventh Circuit reversed the
Tax Court, finding that a hostile takeover can
produce deductible expenses in countering the offer
at the outset, as well as capitalized costs for costs
incurred later to consummate the acquisition. *A.E.
Staley Manufacturing Co. v. Comm'r* (7th Cir.
1997).

This is still an evolving area. However, the 15-
year amortization treatment of I.R.C. § 197 (discussed in § 36.A) cannot be an independent basis
for amortizing such costs in a nontaxable transaction, since it cannot be utilized for "fees for
professional services, and any transaction costs,
incurred by parties to a transaction" for which any
portion of the gain or loss is deferred (I.R.C.
§ 197(e)(8)).

PART III. THE LEGAL POWER AND DUTIES OF BOARDS OF DIRECTORS AND CONTROLLING SHAREHOLDERS IN ACQUISITIONS

CHAPTER 9

THE TARGET BOARD OF DIRECTORS' POWER TO BLOCK TAKEOVERS

Statutory mergers and asset acquisitions require the approval of the target board of directors to proceed. In both types of acquisitions, the target board typically signs an acquisition agreement and recommends ratification by target shareholders. An acquirer must negotiate with the board on acquisition terms (a *negotiated* or *friendly* acquisition). One form of acquisition, a *pure stock* acquisition, does not—in theory—need the approval of the target board of directors to succeed. The acquirer purchases shares directly from the target shareholders, who do not need the approval of the target board to agree to sell their shares. If an acquirer purchases control from target shareholders and the target board does not agree to the transaction, it is a *hostile* acquisition or *hostile takeover*.

Clever firm structural changes and state statutes have all but doomed hostile acquisitions by establishing a practical requirement for target board approval in stock acquisitions. Takeover offers may start hostile, that is, without board approval, but most usually end friendly. The hostile offer is now often used merely to secure bargaining leverage over the target board by inviting target shareholders to pressure their board to accept an acquisition offer. The last remaining truly hostile acquisition is one that first replaces a balking target board through a hostile proxy solicitation and then closes the acquisition with a new, now friendly, board. E.g., *Hilton Hotels Corp. v. ITT Corp.* (D. Nev. 1997) (combination tender offer/proxy contest).

§ 37. Firm-Specific Hostile Takeover Defenses

Firms concerned about reducing their vulnerability to unwanted takeovers have fashioned a growing number of defenses. There are three different kinds of takeover defenses relevant to our study of board power. The categories are defined by the role of shareholders in the creation of each defense: first, takeover defenses that require specific shareholder ratification (e.g., "shark repellent" certificate amendments); second, takeover defenses put in place by the board using very general grants of authority contained in a firm's certificate or articles of incorporation (e.g., a firm uses a charter provision authorizing the issuance of "blank check" preferred stock to promulgate a poison pill plan); and third, take-over defenses based on the board's general powers as granted in a state corporate code (e.g., a board uses a code provision authorizing a board to contract for the sale of firm assets to erect a crown jewel defense). In the first category, shareholders must vote to approve the specific defense in question. In the second category, shareholders, unless the general grant is in a firm's original charter, must vote to amend a firm's charter to give the board the general power. And in the third category, shareholders do not necessarily vote at all, unless they vote to amend a charter to remove the board's power to effectuate the defense.

The shareholders are not powerless, however, with respect to defenses promulgated without specific ratification (categories two and three). They can, using the shareholder resolution procedure provided under SEC Rule 14a-8 (Shareholder Proposals), vote to recommend that a board withdraw specific defenses that it has chosen to put in place. Moreover, a board deciding to use a takeover defense in categories two or three could choose to ask for a positive shareholder ratification, although unnecessary, to protect them from shareholder-derivative litigation.

Shark Repellant Amendments to Certificates or Articles of Incorporation. Certificate amendments that require a specific shareholder vote are called *shark repellent* amendments. Drafters of early shark repellent amendments designed them to retard the ability of someone with newly-acquired voting power from taking control of the firm's board of directors. The amendments provided for a staggered board of directors (only a minority, usually one-third, of the board seats are the subject of an election in any one year), for eliminating shareholder voting through the written consent procedure (a method of voting that does not require a formal shareholders' meeting), for limiting the right of shareholders to call a special meeting of shareholders, for prohibiting the removal of a sitting director unless for cause, for limiting the creation of new seats on the board of directors, and for giving the remaining members of the board the sole authority to appoint new directors if a director resigns in mid-term.

First-generation shark repellent certificate amendments proved to be only marginally effective. Once an acquirer gained voting control of the stock, existing board members owed the new owner fiduciary duties, and most board members who could not respond to the new owner's requests simply resigned rather than continue in an uncomfortable lame duck capacity, at constant risk of being the object of a suit brought by the new controlling shareholder. Moreover, courts prohibited the existing board from finding ways of diluting the ownership of a new controlling owner once the new owner had the controlling block of stock. *Condec Corp. v. Lukenheimer Co.* (Del. Ch. 1967) (the court enjoined the issuance of a large block of new shares to a friendly party after an unwanted buyer had otherwise obtained control).

Lawyers, therefore, designed a second round of certificate amendments with much more punch. The more powerful amendments contain provisions for a super-majority vote for all business combinations between a controlling shareholder and the firm if the controlling shareholder acquired control without the specific approval of a pre-existing board of directors or if the controlling shareholder did not meet fair price criteria in the merger. Some certificate amendments give non-tendering shareholders in hostile acquisitions the right to put their stock to the firm for a specified period of time at a generous price after a successful stock acquisition. Others reduce the voting rights of the acquirer's purchased target stock unless the acquisition meets specified fair price requirements or is approved by non-selling shareholders.

The most extreme form of this sophisticated class of certificate amendments is one that changes the voting rights of outstanding common stock. In *time-phased* voting plans, a firm gives multiple votes per share to all outstanding common shareholders, but the multiple votes disappear on the transfer of the underlying stock and reappear when a shareholder holds the stock for three or four years. In *capped voting* plans, a firm limits the voting power of shares based on the number of shares owned. Shareholders who purchase shares in excess of the triggering amount do not get voting rights on the excess shares.

Finally, a firm can recapitalize, amending their certificate of incorporation to create two classes of common stock (two-tier voting stock). One class, sold exclusively to insiders, has concentrated voting power and diluted rights to the firm's equity (limited dividend and liquidation distribution rights).

Poison Pill Plans. The major disadvantages of certificate amendments adopted by shareholder vote are: first, they take time to put in place; second, they are not flexible; and third, the firm must justify them in comprehensive disclosure documents required by the federal proxy solicitation regulations. In response, clever corporate lawyers designed new defenses that can be implemented without an instantaneous shareholder vote—the firms can employ them in less time and do not have to justify them in proxy statements.

The most popular of these defenses is a *poison pill plan*, a dividend distribution (to existing shareholders) of stock, stock rights or other securities (notes, for example) that have special redemption or conversion provisions. The conversion options in these instruments are activated by an unapproved stock acquisition of a specified percentage of a firm's stock (a trigger) and make the issuer prohibitively expensive to buy.

Most poison pill plans are designed so that no bidder can afford to trigger them with an unapproved stock acquisition. Boards retain the right to waive the effects of a plan, usually through a right to redeem the outstanding securities for a nominal fee. Thus buyers must negotiate with the board before acquiring a triggering block of stock, seeking the board's approval of the acquisition and the board's agreement that it will redeem the outstanding conversion rights. In other words, poison pill plans force bidders to negotiate with the target board in stock acquisitions—acquisitions that the bidder could otherwise consummate without the board's approval.

The poison pill plans, which began as distributions of convertible preferred stock, have evolved into distributions of stock rights (options to purchase stock from the firm) and convertible debt (convertible debentures). Some firms, concerned about the legality of any one plan in a given jurisdiction and hedging their bets, will put in place two or even three plans—each based on a different underlying security. A board, to be able to create one of the popular poison pill plans, must have the authority to issue rights, debt or preferred stock with rights and privileges set by board resolution at the time of issuance.

A charter provision that empowers the board to issue novel kinds of preferred stock is called a *blank check preferred provision.* Most states require an express declaration in a firm's certificate of incorporation that its board can issue preferred stock with rights and privileges set at the time of issuance. E.g., DGCL §§ 102(a)(4) & 151(a). This means that at some point the shareholders must have voted to authorize the blank check provision. On the other hand, most state corporate codes provide that boards have a default power (absent a contrary provision in the certificate) to issue stock rights and to place debt with the terms set by the board at the time of issuance. DGCL §§ 122(13) & 157. So stock rights and convertible debt plans may not require even a general form of shareholder authorization.

Firm Exchange Offers. A second member of this category of defenses, that require general but not specific shareholder authorization, is less popular and more controversial—stock exchange offers or stock dividends that put in place a two-tier voting stock system. In the exchange tender offer, a firm offers stock with diluted voting power and concentrated claims on equity for its outstanding common stock. The insiders do not tender, the outsiders do, and the insiders end up with concentrated voting power. A board must have authorization in its certificate, or must amend the corporation's certificate to grant the board authorization, to issue the non-voting or diluted voting common stock. Again, many publicly-traded firms have amended their certificates to give their boards this authority and even though unused, the provisions are available should the need arise. In stock distributions, a firm issues super voting stock as a stock dividend on its common stock with a transfer restriction that converts the super voting stock to lower voting common stock if the new stock is sold. Insiders hold and outsiders trade.

Lock-ups and Other Asset-Based Strategies. The third category of defenses—those that do not require any shareholder vote, even at the most general level of authorization—is the most wide-ranging. Boards of directors use their inherent power over firm assets to make the firm unattractive to unwanted bidders. These defenses are often less attractive than a poison pill plan, because the defenses in category three usually require that the board expend assets or make major changes in the capital structure of the firm.

The board sells or gives contingent rights to the key firm asset to a third party (the *crown jewel* or *asset lock-up* defense), buys the stock of an unwanted bidder (*greenmail*), gives top managers handsome severance payments contingent on control changes (*golden parachutes*), or issues stock or contingent stock rights (a *stock lock-up*) to a friendly party (a *white squire*) subject to reselling restrictions (a *standstill agreement*). The firm makes acquisitions of its own to create antitrust problems for the bidder, to create national defense concerns if the bidder is foreign (the *Pentagon play*), or to acquire control of the bidder in a reverse acquisition (the *Pac-Man* defense).

The most common modern defense in this category is a radical restructuring, the *leveraged recapitalization*—the target releverages itself by selling debt and passing the cash proceeds of the placement back to its own shareholders in a huge one-time stock dividend. By releveraging, a firm exhausts its debt capacity and its cash reserves so that a bidder cannot use the firm's own assets to finance an acquisition.

§ 38. State Anti-Takeover Statutes

The total count of states with some form of anti-takeover legislation is over 40. There are close to 10 types of statutes in use. Two-thirds of our largest corporations are incorporated in five states, all of which have anti-takeover laws (Delaware, New York, Ohio, Pennsylvania and Massachusetts). Delaware has two state takeover laws: a three-year freeze-out statute and a succession of labor contract provisions. The other four states have some of the most extensive and innovative defensive takeover regulations in the country. Most states that have anti-takeover statutes have more than one type. Pennsylvania, for example, has a control share act, a business combination statute, a poison pill statute, a severance pay statute, a redemption statute and a disgorgement statute.

Most state legislatures attempting to regulate tender offers rely on one or more of four types of statutes: control share acquisitions statutes, fair price provision statutes, right of redemption statutes and business combination statutes.

In a *control share* statute, a bidder not approved by the board of directors cannot vote the newly-acquired shares without a favorable vote of the remaining shareholders. See, e.g., Ind. Code Ann. § 23-1-42 (Burns Supp. 1986); Minn. Stat. Ann. § 302A.671 (West 1985 & Supp.1987); Mo. Ann. Stat. § 351.407 (Vernon Supp. 1987); Ohio Rev. Code Ann. §§ 1701.831 (Anderson 1985). In a *fair price* statute, a bidder not approved by the board cannot merge its firm into the target unless the remaining target shareholders are paid a fair price (the price paid any other shareholder for a period of time prior to the merger) or a majority of them approve. See, e.g., Md. Corps. & Ass'ns Code Ann. §§ 3-601 to -603 (1985 & Supp. 1986). In a *redemption* statute, also known as an *appraisal* statute, shareholders receive a put right for fair value of their shares contingent on a triggering stock acquisition. See, e.g., Pa. Stat. Ann. tit. 15 §§ 1408(B), 1409(C), 1910 (Purdon Supp. 1986); Me. Rev. Stat. Ann. tit. 13-A, § 910 (Supp. 1986); Utah Code Ann. § 16-10-76.5 (Supp. 1986). In *business combination* statutes, also known as *freeze-out* statutes, the acquirer may not engage in a back-end merger (or its equivalent) for a period of years after a triggering stock acquisition not approved by the target board. Ind. Code Ann. § 23-1-43 (Burns

Supp. 1986); Ky. Rev. Stat. Ann. § 271A.397(3) (Baldwin Supp. 1986); Mo. Ann. Stat. § 351.459 (Vernon Supp. 1987); N.Y. Bus. Corp. L. § 912(a)(5) (McKinney 1986).

Less popular statutes include Pennsylvania's *disgorgement* (or anti-greenmail) statute in which an unsuccessful hostile bidder, seeking to sell shares to a successful bidder, must give all profits back to the target firm. One also sees *severance* statutes in which a successful hostile bidder must offer lucrative severance packages to target employees.

The Supreme Court of the United States has held that control share acts do not violate the commerce or supremacy clauses of the United States Constitution (*CTS Corp. v. Dynamics Corp.* (U.S. 1987)) and federal circuit courts have extended the reasoning of the opinion to cover the other popular statutes. See, e.g., *WLR Foods v. Tyson Foods* (4th Cir. 1995) (Virginia's four statutes).

The most important statutory reaction to takeovers is the business combination statute. First enacted by New York, and most recently by Delaware, this type of statute prohibits certain business combinations between an interested shareholder and the target corporation for an extended period of time—five years in the case of New York's statute and three years in Delaware's § 203. DGCL § 203. The statutes stop most leveraged or financial takeovers because a back-end merger (between the acquisition vehicle and the target) is necessary to get control over the assets of the target (to attach debt in the acquisition vehicle to the target's assets, to sell assets to generate cash and so on—no back-end merger, no LBO).

Business combination statutes typically contain exceptions allowing for friendly offerors to consummate post-takeover transactions. Common examples include board approval, or board approval plus a vote of a super-majority of the stockholders. Business combination restrictions shield shareholders from the coerciveness of front-end loaded, two-tier offers by preventing the offeror from effecting the second step of the offer unless the target's board of directors and, in some instances, the target's shareholders, approve the transaction.

Delaware's statute encompasses a variety of transactions between a stockholder and the corporation of whose outstanding voting stock the stockholder owns at least 15 percent. The full statute, put simply, prevents business combinations, broadly defined, between an interested stockholder (basically a 15 percent owner of the outstanding voting stock of the corporation) and the target corporation for a three-year period, unless one of the exceptions to the statute applies. Subsection (a) of § 203 sets forth three ways an interested stockholder otherwise subject to the section may escape its moratorium on business combinations. Subsection (b) lists circumstances in which the section will not apply at all.

Subsection (a) allows a tender offeror to consummate a second-step merger or other business combination where: (1) the board approves the combination prior to the date the offeror becomes an interested stockholder; (2) the transaction which transforms the stockholder into an interested stockholder results in the interested stockholder owning at least 85 percent of the outstanding voting stock, excluding, for the purposes of calculating that percentage, shares owned by officers who are also directors and certain employee stock plans; (3) the board of directors approves the business combination after the person becomes an interested stockholder and the proposed combination is authorized by two-thirds of the outstanding voting stock not owned by the interested stockholder.

Subsection (b) lists six circumstances in which § 203 will not apply. Subsection (b)(1) permits newly-organized corporations to exempt themselves from the statute. Subsection (b)(2) gave the board of directors of a Delaware corporation until May 3, 1988, to amend the corporation's bylaws to *opt out* of the coverage of the statute. The third subparagraph, (b)(3), gives stockholders the power to amend the corporation's bylaws or certificate of incorporation in order to place the corporation outside the statute. Such an amendment will not be effective for 12 months, however. Further, a successful offeror is forbidden from using a stock-holder amendment opt-out. Only persons who become interested stockholders after the amendment may take advantage of it. Subsection (b)(4) exempts certain small companies not listed on a national exchange, quoted through a national securities association, or with fewer than 2,000 stockholders. The fifth subsection provides that persons who become interested stockholders inadvertently, e.g., through gift or inheritance, are not bound by § 203. The sixth subsection of 203(b) releases a bidder from combination restrictions when management—or a third party approved by management—proposes a merger, sale of substantial assets, or tender or exchange offer for more than 50 percent of the outstanding voting stock. In that event, the bidder may devise a competing proposal within 20 days of the announcement of the management-endorsed proposal. This exception allows stockholders an opportunity to consider competing bids.

The Delaware statute, like most state antitakeover statutes (excepting the appraisal statute in Pennsylvania), does not present a substantial additional deterrent to hostile takeovers; it adds yet another defensive weapon to an already potent arsenal of defenses—poison pill plans and second-generation shark repellant amendments. Before the adoption of the statute, the Delaware courts had been faced with supervising the decisions of target boards in creating and holding onto poison pill plans; the statute does not materially change their responsibility. The Delaware courts must now decide—under their increasingly intricate edifice of fiduciary duty case law—legal challenges both to a board's decision not to waive a firm-specific poison pill plan and its decision not to waive the statutory three-year cooling-off period.

§ 39. Court Review of a Board's Decision to Block Hostile Takeovers

When frustrated bidders or target shareholders contest a target's anti-takeover defense in court, there are two separate legal issues. First, are the defenses void *ab initio* as outside the power of the board of directors to adopt? And, second, if the defenses are *prima facie* valid, have the directors abused their discretion (breached their fiduciary duty to their share-holders) in deploying or refusing to defuse a defense on the facts of a particular case? State anti-takeover statutes have considerably narrowed the range of the first question. Even when state legislation does not create or authorize the defense, courts have now largely left the field to the defending corporations, with one very important exception (defenses based on restricting share-holder voting rights), and look hard at only the second question.

A. Void Defenses

There are two lines of Delaware cases that invalidate some defenses without regard to their specific use in a particular takeover. Both relate to the ability of a hostile bidder to wage a successful proxy contest for control of the board.

In *Quickturn Design Systems v. Shapiro* (Del. 1998), the Delaware Supreme Court held invalid a poison pill plan that could not be waived by a newly-elected board for six months after their election. The court said the plan was an infringement of the board's statutory power to manage the affairs of the firm. The drafters of the plan intended to stop hostile proxy solicitations for control of the board as a prelude to an acquisition. Even if the acquirer took control of the board, the new board could not authorize an acquisition for six months. Stronger versions of the defense, *dead hand* provisions that completely disable the new board from ever waiving a poison pill, are also presumably void.

The second line of cases, based on *Blasius Indus. v. Atlas Corp.* (Del. 1988), invalidates any takeover defense that impairs target shareholders right to vote unless the board can show a compelling justification. Thus a bylaw amendment, adopted by the target board, that increased the shareholder vote needed to amend the bylaws to a 60-percent super-majority, when insiders held nearly 25 percent of the stock, was invalid. *Chesapeake Corporation v. Shore* (Del. Ch. 2000). Similarly, any poison pill plan triggered by a hostile proxy solicitation (as opposed to a hostile stock acquisition) is also void.

B. The Basic Standard for Evaluating the Use of Defenses

The general rule for evaluating the liability of directors sued by unhappy shareholders is the business judgment rule. The court will not substitute its judgment for the boards. *Unitrin, Inc. v. American General Corp.* (Del. 1995) (note 10). The rule in application means that the board is not liable for ordinary negligence; it must be grossly negligent. To get the benefit of the business judgment rule, a board must not act primarily to protect their positions and must act in good faith (free from conflicts of interest) and have acquired an appropriate amount of information on the matters in issue. See *Smith v. Van Gorkom* (Del. 1985).

In *Unocal Corp. v. Mesa Petroleum Co.* (Del. 1985), the Delaware Supreme Court fashioned a special application of the business judgment rule for takeovers. The board's conduct must satisfy a two-threshold test before the business judgment rule applies. The first part is the *reasonableness* test (the board has reasonable grounds for believing an offer represents a threat to corporate welfare) and the second part is the *proportionality* test (the board's defensive response is not draconian and inappropriate to the threat, that is, within a range of reasonableness). If the board does not satisfy the threshold tests, its conduct is evaluated under the *entire fairness* test. It is rare but possible for directors to satisfy this test even without the protection of the business judgment rule.

If a target board favors one bidder over another, a specialized application of the *Unocal* two-part threshold test applies. First articulated in *Revlon v. MacAndrews* (Del. 1986), the board must satisfy the reasonableness test and the proportionality test in its decision to disadvantage one bidder and favor another.

In *Unitrin*, the board repurchased its own stock to consolidate the voting power of insiders and take advantage of a super-voting provision in the firm's charter. The board consequently adopted a poison pill plan. The Chancery Court upheld the poison pill plan but rejected the repurchase program. The Supreme Court remanded, suggesting that the Chancery Court reconsider its judgment on the repurchase program. On the facts, the threat was an inadequate, coercive offer. The first part of the test seems to be much more important than the second; once a court agrees with the board that a bidder was a threat, then defenses are easy to justify. At issue in the case, however, was the second half of the threshold—the proportionality test. In applying the proportionality test, one sees the sensitivity of the Delaware courts to the effect of tender offer defenses on proxy contests. Would the repurchase program preclude a proxy contest? If so, the defense might be draconian and void. The Chancery Court said yes, the bidder was chilled from buying stock to mount a proxy fight; the Supreme Court said no. In a proxy contest, the Supreme Court found the bidder could, even after the repurchase program, solicit enough other shareholders to obtain control, largely held by institutional investors.

In *Paramount Communications v. Time* (Del. 1989), the high-water mark of takeover defenses, the court held that the defenses to a takeover by Paramount were reasonable because the board of Time reasonably believed that Paramount's offer threatened a previously-negotiated combination between Time and Warner. Time also wanted to protect the "Time culture." The Time board, to protect its shareholders, disenfranchised them— the Time shareholders were not allowed to vote on the Time/Warner combination. The Time board turned a statutory merger with Warner into a cash tender offer for Warner and blocked the Paramount offer. The court upheld the Time board's refusal entertain the Paramount bid. The result in the case is perhaps the most criticized of all the Delaware takeover cases.

In *Shamrock Holdings v. Polaroid Corp.* (Del. Ch. 1989), the Polaroid board was anticipating a huge court judgment against a third party, Kodak, and could not reveal to their shareholders all the information necessary for them to value accurately their stock in their decision on whether to accept the Shamrock bid. The threat to the company was an unwitting, bargain sale to a bidder and justified a defense. If a firm has insider information that cannot be disclosed until it is less sensitive, then a takeover defense is in the best interests of current shareholders.

C. State Legislation Modifying the Basic Fiduciary Standards

Liability Limitations in the Certification of Incorporation. Section § 102(b)(7) in the Delaware General Corporation Law authorizes corporations to put in their certificates of incorporation a provision

> eliminating or limiting the personal liability of a director to the corporation or its shareholders for monetary damages for breach of fiduciary duty as a director, provided that such provision shall not eliminate or limit the liability of a director; (i) For any breach of the director's duty of loyalty to the corporation or its stockholders; (ii) for acts or omissions not in good faith or which involve intentional misconduct or a knowing violation of law; (iii) under section 174 of this title [Unlawful Distributions]; or (iv) for any transaction from which the director derived an improper personal benefit....

Over 40 states have adopted a version of the Delaware provision. Most publicly-traded firms have accepted the invitation of the statute and passed charter amendments waiving director liability to the full extent allowed under the provision. In a sense, the section represents the ultimate shark repellent amendment. The Model Business Corporation Act has a stronger version of the Delaware section in § 2.02(b)(4) (there is no reservation for a breach of the duty of loyalty, and the reservation for intentional misconduct does not include as an alternative ground a lack of good faith). MBCA § 2.02 (b)(4).

In the two *Arnold v. Society for Savings Bancorp* opinions, (Del. 1994) and (Del. 1996), the Delaware Supreme Court demonstrated that it will parse the allegations and facts carefully in cases involving the board's adoption and use of takeover defenses. The court will apply § 102(b)(7) to some allegations and not others, depending on whether the court classifies the claim as one for a breach of a duty of care or loyalty. The courts in a state adopting the MBCA language need only classify the claim as not alleging personal gain or intentional misconduct.

Constituency Statutes. These state statutes authorize boards to consider non-financial matters and constituencies other than shareholders in deciding whether to accept a takeover offer. Nearly 30 states have adopted some version of a constituency statute. Significantly, Delaware has as yet refused to adopt any version of the constituency statutes and the drafters of the Model Business Corporation Act have refused to put such a provision in their Model Act.

Constituency statutes in several states—e.g., Connecticut, Iowa, Louisiana, Missouri, Oregon and Tennessee—apply only to change-of-control contests and the rest apply to all board decisions. Most constituency statutes permit directors to *consider* the interests of constituencies other than shareholders—typically employees, creditors, suppliers, customers and communities, among others (other *stakeholders*)—and a few allow for consideration of the national and state economies. Cf., *Herald Co. v. Seawell* (10th Cir. 1972) (taking into account public interest in sale of locally-owned newspaper to New York publishing chain).

Some permissive statutes contain simply a laundry list of groups, including shareholders, whose interests a board *may* consider. A second type of constituency statute is more directive. Two statutes, those of Indiana and Pennsylvania, direct that a board ought not to consider the interests of any one group (an oblique reference to shareholders) as dominant. Ind. Code § 23-1-35-1(d); Pa. Bus. Corp. L. § 1715. And Connecticut's statute mandates that the board *shall* consider interests of non-shareholder groups. Conn. Gen. Stat. § 33-133(e).

CHAPTER 10

THE BOARD OF DIRECTORS'
DECISION TO SELL THE FIRM

The Delaware Supreme Court uses three basic tests for judging the actions of a selling firm's board in an acquisition: the basic *business judgment rule* applied in *Smith v. Van Gorkom* (Del. 1985); the *enhanced scrutiny test* (or *Unocal* test*),* applied to auctions when a seller favors one bidder over another, as in *Revlon v. MacAndrews* (Del. 1986); and the *intrinsic fairness test,* applied when directors are operating under conflicts of interest. E.g., *Mills Acquisition Co. v. Macmillan, Inc.* (Del. 1989); *Cede & Co. v. Technicolor* (Del. 1996). Other states tend to follow the lead of the Delaware courts.

§ 40. The Basic Standard for Court Review of a Board's Decision to Sell a Firm to a Single Suitor

In *Smith v. Van Gorkom*, the Delaware Supreme Court stated that, under appropriate circumstances, it would apply the business judgment rule to evaluate the conduct of the board of directors of the selling corporation in a negotiated acquisition. If the rule applies, the board's business decisions are protected from second-guessing by a court. The decisions must be grossly negligent or reckless for board members to be liable.

The business judgment rule does not apply if there is proof of fraud, bad faith or self-dealing (a conflict of interest), or uninformed decision making. Cases in which there are conflicts of interest are termed *duty-of-loyalty* cases. Cases that do not involve fraud or conflicts of interest are termed *duty-of-care* cases. If the business judgment rule is not available, the court evaluates the merits of the deal under the *entire* or *intrinsic fairness test*. The deal must be entirely fair to the shareholders. The details of the entire fairness test are discussed in § 42.

On the facts of *Van Gorkom*, the court found that the selling board had not made an informed decision. The initial board meeting in which the board decided to sell the company was held on short notice, was concluded very quickly, and featured only a brief, oral recommendation from the target CEO and a lukewarm, general endorsement from the target CFO.

The *Van Gorkom* case led to a change in board procedures for selling the company. Most target boards now require one-page *fairness opinions* from independent investment bankers on whether the price offered is within a range of fairness. Moreover, most boards hold lengthy meetings to gather information from both inside and outside experts on the merits of the offer before the board will vote to accept any offer.

Firms may, however, use the liability limitation charter amendments discussed in § 39.B to narrow the scope of a board's liability in duty-of-care cases to reckless or intentional misbehavior. The charter amendments do not affect a board's liability in duty-of-loyalty cases. Those courts in states with constituency statutes may also apply different standards. In Delaware, a state without a constituency statute, the board does not have a fiduciary duty to debt holders, for example. See *Metropolitan Life Ins. v. RJR Nabisco* (S.D.N.Y. 1989). In those states with constituency statutes, a board may consider the interests of other constituencies in a sale.

Deal Protection Measures and Fiduciary Out Clauses. Negotiated merger agreements often contain *deal protection measures* that serve two purposes. First, they provide some economic compensation to the jilted purchaser in the event that the target chooses not to close. Second, the measures obstruct disruption of the deal by another purchaser. Common covenants include the following measures: (1) a limitation on the target corporation's providing confidential information to other potential purchasers (a *no-talk* clause); (2) a limitation on the target corporation's soliciting offers from other potential purchasers (a *no-shop* clause); (3) a requirement that the target managers and directors use their best efforts to close the merger; and (4) a termination fee compensating the purchaser if the transaction does not close (a *goodbye kiss*). Occasionally one also sees (5) a covenant that the target managers will recommend to their shareholders that they approve the deal and will call a shareholder meeting to ratify the transaction or (6) an option granted to the purchaser to acquire stock or assets of the target if the deal does not close (a *lock-up option*).

The deal protection measures are often softened by *fiduciary out* clauses that provide target corporations with an escape hatch. The provision protects the directors of a target company from having to choose between violating their fiduciary obligation to shareholders and violating a purchase agreement. Under the language of a fiduciary out provision, the directors are excused from any action that would constitute a violation of their fiduciary duty. For example, such a clause would allow a target board to negotiate with a third party despite a no-shop clause or waive the requirement that a board recommend a deal to its shareholders. As a check on the breadth of the clause, buyers may demand language requiring that the target board receive an opinion of outside counsel stating that any action foregone under the authority of the clause would constitute a breach of fiduciary duty.

At issue is whether fiduciary out clauses are required by law or a merely an optional contractual provision. During a one-month period in the fall of 1999, three different Chancellors of the Delaware Court of Chancery handed down three opinions on deal protection measures with conflicting signals. See *ACE Limited v. Capital Re Corp.* (Del. Ch. 1999) (as revised March 14, 2000); *Phelps Dodge Corp. v. Cyprus Amax Minerals Co.* (Del. Ch. 1999); *In re IXC Communications v. Cincinnati Bell* (Del. Ch. 1999). The results of the cases are very fact specific. Fiduciary outs do not seem to be required in every merger agreement, but courts may set aside deal protections that do not have fiduciary outs if a target board signs a merger agreement without a thorough investigation of whether there are other potential purchasers in the market.

§ 41. Court Review of a Board's Decision to Sell When There Are Multiple Bidders

The *Revlon v. MacAndrews & Forbes Holdings* (Del. 1986) and *Paramount Communications v. QVC Network* (Del. 1994) cases confront the issue of when and how a target board can favor one bidder over another in an auction for a firm. A target board could, to determine the outcome of a bidding contest for the firm, waive takeover defenses for one bidder but not others.

As an initial issue, a court must determine whether a firm has put itself up for sale. In *QVC Network*, the court found that Paramount had put itself up for sale, unlike Time in the earlier case of

Paramount v. Time (Del. 1989), in which the court held that Time had not put itself up for sale in agreeing to a negotiated merger with Warner. (Paramount lost both cases, each case on the opposite side of the argument.) A corporation puts itself up for sale when it initiates an active bidding process, when it initiates a bust-up of the company's divisions, or when it initiates a transaction that results in a change of control. A change of control occurs when a majority block of stock ends up under the control of a single individual (or small group of individuals), as in the facts of *QVC Network*. A change of control does not occur, however, merely because a diffuse body of shareholders of the purchasing party in a merger ends up with a majority of the stock in the surviving entity, as occurred in *Paramount v. Time* and *Arnold I*.

Once a firm has put itself up for sale, the standard for favoring one bidder over another is high. The firm must meet the entire fairness test, which usually means it must sell to the highest bidder (for its voting shares), unless the board's actions can satisfy a modified *Unocal* standard (the two-part reasonableness/proportionality test). See dicta in *Unitrin v. American General Corp.* (Del. 1995). As demonstrated by the facts of *Revlon*, this test is difficult to satisfy. A board decision to protect the interests of debt holders at the expense of shareholders will not satisfy the test. An example that may satisfy the test occurs when a target board reasonably believes that the financial ability of one of the bidders to pay for the target is suspect.

When a target corporation is in what lawyers now refer to as the *Revlon* zone, the Delaware courts will analyze the board of directors' conduct using an enhanced level of scrutiny that focuses on whether the directors acted reasonably in obtaining the best value for target shareholders. The *QVC* case explained that a target enters the zone when it is to be broken up (a classic LBO or MBO) or when it is sold for cash or to a person or group that will control the acquiring corporation's stock after the acquisition (a change of control). Outside the *Revlon* zone, the Delaware courts will evaluate the activities of the board of directors of the target using the less rigorous and highly deferential business judgment rule. See *Paramount Communications v. Time.*

Consider the effect of the dichotomy. If one publicly-traded company acquires another in a stock-for-stock deal, the business judgment rule applies; if the acquiring company pays in cash (or debt), the enhanced *Revlon* duties apply. If the transaction is structured to give target shareholders a choice of stock or cash, *Revlon* duties apply. See, e.g., *In re Lukens, Inc. Shareholders Litigation* (Del. Ch. 1999) (62 percent of the consideration was cash and 38 percent stock in the acquirer).

Deal Protection Measures. The application of the dichotomy gets fuzzy when applied to deal protection measures (see § 40). Some practitioners believe that Delaware courts will evaluate deal protection measures under the enhanced scrutiny test only if a target is in the *Revlon* zone; that is, Delaware courts will evaluate deal protection measures in stock swap deals under the business judgment rule. The practical effect, for example, is for practitioners to use fiduciary out clauses routinely in deal protection measures when the target is in the *Revlon* zone and more sparsely when a target is outside the zone.

This view may be in error. Since deal protection measures in stock swap acquisitions deter unwanted bids, a traditional *Unocal* analysis may apply. See Leo E. Strine, Jr., "Categorical Confusion: Deal Protection Measures in Stock for Stock Merger Agreements," 56 *Bus. Law.* 919 (2001) (a Vice Chancellor on the Delaware Court of Chancery). Thus the court may evaluate a board's decision to engage in a stock swap merger under the business judgment rule and yet also evaluate the board's decision to use deal protections under the enhanced scrutiny test. Chancellor Strine tells attorneys not to worry, the enhanced scrutiny test on such facts will not have the rigor of full *Revlon* duties. Under the enhanced scrutiny test,

> well-motivated directors ought to have the right to present a strategic merger to their stockholders and to give their merger partner substantial contractual protections to induce them to contract. Unlike in the Revlon context,

the court will defer to director decisions to give a preferred merger partner bidding and timing advantages over later emerging rivals. This deference to directors, as a practical matter, may mean that courts will give scant weight to whether deal protection measures are preclusive of other bids as a short-term matter. That is, if all that the board is asking for is to go first and to require other bidders to await the outcome of an unfettered stockholder vote, it seems likely to get that opportunity.

Id. at 941-42.

Effect of Constituency Statutes. Note, however, that in those states that have adopted constituency statutes (and Delaware has not), a case with the facts of the *Revlon* case may be decided differently. See § 39.C. A court in New York could decide that the Revlon board's decision to support its debenture holders was within the board authority under the New York version of a constituency statute. See, e.g., *Norfolk Southern Corp. v. Conrail* (E.D. Pa. 1996) (unpublished opinion), aff'd (3d Cir. 1997) (supporting the decision of the board of a railroad corporation to favor one bidder over another in the national interest).

§ 42. Court Review of a Board's Decision to Sell When Managers Are Buyers (MBOs)

When a target's senior managers, board members or controlling shareholders have major stakes in the acquiring firm, the courts take a much closer look at the transaction. In acquisitions in which senior managers are on both sides of the deal, there is a conflict of interest and the business judgment rule is unavailable. The board's decision must then meet the entire or intrinsic fairness test.

If the plaintiff alleges a conflict of interest, the burden of proof shifts to the defendants. If the defendants can prove that fully-informed shareholders ratified a board's decision or that a board delegated decision-making power to a subcommittee of disinterested directors (a Special Committee) that acted independently and with adequate information, the burden of proof shifts from the defendants to the plaintiffs to prove lack of entire fairness. The Delaware courts have held that the test does not morph into the business judgment rule once the board sanitizes the decision makers, as many had thought for a time.

In *Weinberger v. UOP* (Del. 1983), the Delaware Supreme Court applied the intrinsic fairness test to a squeeze-out (or cash-out) merger. (In a squeeze-out merger, a majority shareholder eliminates the minority shareholders.) The court explained the entire fairness test as having two parts, an investigation into the procedure of the deal (*fair procedure*) and an investigation into the deal price (*fair price*). In this case the court held that the procedure was not fair because members of the target, subsidiary board who were also officers of the parent, acquiring corporation, used their special access to target company information to the advantage of the acquirer. The court also noted in dicta its support for a legitimate Special Committee decision-making structure for the target.

In *Mills Acquisition v. Macmillan* (Del. 1989), the Special Committee ran a rigged auction between a leveraged buy-out group that included senior managers of the target (a classic MBO, management buy-out) and an independent bidder. The committee tipped the MBO group on the content of its competitor's bids. The court held that the Special Committee's actions did not meet the entire fairness test.

CHAPTER 11

THE LEGAL DUTIES OF CONTROLLING SHAREHOLDERS IN ACQUISITIONS

§ 43. The Obligation to Share the Proceeds from the Sale of a Controlling Block of Stock

A. No General Duty to Share Sale Proceeds from Sale of Controlling Block of Stock

The general rule in the common law is that a controlling shareholder who sells her block of stock and thereby control in a corporation does not have to share any part of the sale proceeds with the minority shareholders or otherwise give the minority shareholders an opportunity to participate in the stock sale. *Zetlin v. Hanson Holdings* (N.Y. 1979). This is true even if the controlling shareholder receives a control premium for her shares. (If the stock is trading at $100 a share and the price for a 51 percent controlling block of shares is $130 a share, the control premium is $30 a share.) A maverick Second Circuit case, *Perlman v. Feldman* (2d Cir. 1954) (sale during war time price controls), often featured in basic corporations courses, has been limited to its unique facts. See, e.g., *Mendel v. Carroll* (Del. Ch. 1994).

Yet the SEC has established an equal treatment rule of sorts for tender offers in SEC Rule 14d-10. A public tender offer for over 5 percent of registered voting stock in a public company must include all shareholders; it cannot include, for example, only the large institutional shareholders. Moreover, the offeror in a public tender offer cannot purchase shares privately once the tender offer has begun.

B. The Duty Not to Usurp a Corporate Opportunity

The *corporate opportunity doctrine*, the duty of senior managers not to usurp business opportunities that belong to the firm, can apply to acquisitions. In the classic case a purchaser approaches a CEO and asks to buy the firm. The CEO, rather than sell the company, offers to sell the purchaser the CEO's personal controlling block of stock. This violates the corporate opportunity doctrine. *Thorpe v. CERBCO* (Del. 1996). In *Thorpe*, the purchaser wanted to purchase a subsidiary from another corporation. The officers of the parent corporation convinced the purchaser to buy their controlling stock in the parent instead. As often happens, the officers lied to their board about the purchaser's interest in the sub. In an odd twist, the officers had the voting power, however, to block any sale of the sub to the purchaser. The voting power of the officers meant that the corporation could not take advantage of any purchase offer and that the officers therefore did not usurp a corporate opportunity. The court held that the officers' actions violated their fiduciary duty, however.

§ 44. The Obligation Not to Harm the Remaining Shareholders by Selling to a Looter

California courts have pioneered a duty of a majority shareholder not to sell to someone known, or who should be known, to be a *looter*. *Debaun v. First Western Bank and Trust Co.* (Cal. Ct. App. 1975). The Delaware Chancery Court seems to have accepted the rule as well. *Harris v. Carter* (Del. Ch. 1990). In *Debaun*, the selling controlling shareholder had seen an unfavorable Dunn & Bradstreet report on the purchaser and the structure of the sale was fishy. Installment payments on the purchase price were to be made out of corporate distributions (an *earnout* provision) that were larger than the firm's after-tax profits.

§ 45. No Pure Sales of a Corporate Office

A controlling shareholder may not agree with a purchaser to sell a board position in the company unless the agreement is accompanied by a sale of effective control of the company itself. *Essex Universal Corp. v. Yates* (2d Cir. 1962). In the case, a 28-percent shareholder sold his block of stock with the understanding that he would cause a majority of the board to resign one at a time, with the remaining directors agreeing to appoint new directors, one at a time, selected by the purchaser. The court held that the contract provision was legal as long as the stock represented effective control of the firm. If the seller did not have effective control, the contract was an illegal sale of a pure corporate office. The dissent said that the stock had to represent legal control, 51 percent, otherwise the shareholders were deprived of their right to vote on the election of directors.

CHAPTER 12

THE FIDUCIARY DUTY OF FINANCIAL CONSULTANTS IN ACQUISITIONS: INVESTMENT BANKERS

When a purchasing company pays too much for another company and the combined company fails soon after the acquisition, ending up in bankruptcy, the bankruptcy trustee, looking for deep pockets to satisfy unpaid creditors, often sues the purchasing company's investment banker. The failure is usually caused by the inability of the combined company to pay off the huge new debts incurred in the acquisition financing.

Investment bankers can play many roles in a transaction. On the facts of *In re Daisy Systems Corp.* (9th Cir. 1996), for example, the investment banker and the purchaser executed an engagement letter with two subsequent amendments. Initially the investment banker was an advisor on information gathered by the company (with no independent verification by the bank). When the target refused to sell and the purchasing company decided to make a hostile bid for cash, the investment banker then agreed to be the deal manager and help secure deal financing. Thereafter the investment banker agreed to be an underwriter of debt securities sold to finance the acquisition and to provide a highly confident letter on the financing behind a tender offer. When other banks refused to lend money to finance the tender offer, the investment bank offered to be the primary lender. When the deal turns friendly and the parties sign a merger agreement, an investment bank usually writes a fairness opinion for the seller on the adequacy of the deal price (the *Daisy* opinion is silent here). See § 40.

In *Daisy* the bankruptcy trustee sued the investment bank alleging negligence (professional malpractice), negligent misrepresentation and a breach of fiduciary duty. The court granted summary judgment on the negligent misrepresentation claim but let the other two claims proceed to trial. The court held that the breach of fiduciary duty claim would depend on whether the investment bank understood that the CEO of the purchasing company lacked sophistication and was relying heavily on the judgment of the bank. The dissent would have also granted summary judgment on the fiduciary duty claim.

PART IV.   OTHER REGULATIONS AFFECTING ACQUISITIONS

CHAPTER 13

ANTITRUST LEGISLATION ON ACQUISITIONS

Consumer protection in acquisitions has been a central part of the American legal landscape since the late 1800s. Industrial combinations after the Civil War demonstrated one form of opportunistic behavior in acquisitions: Two competing firms combine, creating a single firm that has enough market power to engage in noncompetitive pricing, or enough size to collude with other major firms to fix prices through express or tacit agreements. The surviving firm in such a combination may be more profitable than the two constituent firms standing separately, but this occurs at the expense of the consumers, who pay higher prices. The firms, in bargaining over the merger price, simply split the expected gains created by monopolistic or oligopolistic pricing behavior.

A federal antitrust statute known as the Clayton Act, 15 U.S.C. § 12 et seq., and state antitrust statutes modeled after the Clayton Act, are designed to deter such acquisitions.

§ 46. The Clayton Act of 1914

The Clayton Act of 1914 (as amended by the Celler-Kefauver Anti-Merger Act of 1950) expands on the general prohibitions of the Sherman Act of 1890 and is intended to stop anti-competitive problems in their incipiency by regulating acquisitions. Section 7 of the Clayton Act, 15 U.S.C. § 18, prohibits any merger or acquisition of stock or assets "where in any line of commerce or in any activity affecting commerce in any section of the country, the effect of such acquisition may be substantially to lessen competition, or to tend to create a monopoly." Section 15 of the Clayton Act empowers the Attorney General, and § 13(b) of the Federal Trade Commission Act empowers the FTC to seek a court order enjoining consummation of a merger that would violate § 7. In addition, the Commission may seek a cease and desist order in an administrative proceeding against a merger under either § 11 of the Clayton Act or § 5 of the FTC Act, or both. Private parties may also seek injunctive relief under 15 U.S.C. § 26.

There is a special statute for research and development joint ventures, the National Cooperative Research and Production Act, that is less confining to these R&D combinations than the

Clayton Act would be if it were applied. 15 U.S.C. § 4301 et seq.

Congress designed the Clayton Act language to be preemptive—to prohibit acquisitions that "may...substantially lessen competition." The government may stop acquisitions even if they do not in fact lessen competition. The case law on the Clayton Act analyzes mergers in three categories: horizontal (between competitors), vertical (between suppliers and customers), and conglomerate (between firms in unrelated markets). The law is the most developed on horizontal mergers, has recently reversed field on vertical mergers and is uncertain when applied to conglomerates.

The Department of Justice (in cooperation with with the FTC), struggling with the general language and with judges who do not cooperate with official views of that language, issued formal guidelines on enforcement policy for horizontal mergers in 1992. DOJ and FTC, 1992 Horizontal Merger Guidelines.

The Guidelines start with a formula and soften its results with selected market considerations. The formula uses the Herfindahl-Hirschman Index (HHI) of concentration. To apply the formula, one 1) defines a market, 2) calculates the market shares of the parties to an acquisition and all the other competitors, and 3) then sums the squares of the individual market shares of all the participants. This is done twice, once assuming no acquisition and then assuming the acquisition in issue.

If the HHI before the acquisition is over 1800, the market is highly concentrated; if the HHI is between 1000 and 1800, the market is moderately concentrated; below 1000 the market is not concentrated. In the highly-concentrated market, if the acquisition adds over 50 points to the index, it raises "significant competitive concerns"; in the moderately-concentrated market, if the acquisition adds over 100 points it raises "significant competitive concerns."

The soft information that the agency uses to mitigate what the HHI numbers otherwise indicate includes recent market conditions (Is the market growing?), the ease of entry of new firms into the market, the health of the parties to the acquisition (Is one of the parties otherwise likely to go belly up?), and the efficiencies in operation generated by the acquisition (Are the price reductions due to reduced production costs?).

The cases on the Clayton Act demonstrate that the factual definition of the relevant product market often determines the result. The plaintiffs attempt to narrow the size of the relevant market and the defendants attempt to expand it. Once the product market is defined, the market concentration figures follow mathematically. In *Community Publishers v. DR Partners* (8th Cir. 1998), for example, after the court knocked the national and state papers out of the relevant market and limited the market to local daily newspapers in northwest Arkansas, a local newspaper merger was doomed.

§ 47. The Hart-Scott-Rodino Antitrust Improvements Act of 1976

The Hart-Scott-Rodino Antitrust Improvements Act of 1976 (HSR Act) grew out of the frustration of the Department of Justice in its attempt to enjoin mergers in lawsuits that lasted over five years. Often the mergers had been long closed and were impossible to unscramble. So Congress passed a notification act that requires all parties of acquisitions of any size to notify the DOJ and the FTC of any pending merger plans. Note the double dipping: The Clayton Act proscribes mergers that may lessen competition and HSR requires notification of mergers that might violate the Clayton Act. After notification, there is a mandated waiting period before any deal closes.

The notification requirements include a size-of-transaction test and a size-of-party test. The parties must file if one party, with total assets or net sales of $100 million or more, is acquiring voting securities or assets of another party with total assets (or net sales if a manufacturer) of $10 million or more and the transaction is valued at more than $50 million. The parties to all transactions valued at over $200 million must file regardless of the size of the parties involved or the percentage of the stock or assets acquired.

Exempted transactions include goods or realty transferred in the ordinary course of business, acquisitions of 10 percent or less of the voting securities of a seller solely for the purpose of investment, acquisitions by institutional investors and specified acquisitions of foreign issuers.

To implement the statutory standards the FTC has, by administrative rule, created "notification thresholds." The thresholds require filings for acquisitions of assets and voting securities valued at greater than $50 million but less than $100 million, $100 million or greater but less than $500 million, and $500 million or greater. There are separate thresholds for acquisitions of voting securities amounting to 25 percent of the issuer's outstanding voting securities if valued at more than $1 billion and of voting securities amounting to 50 percent of the issuer's outstanding voting securities if valued at more than $50 million. The acquiring party identifies which of these acquisition thresholds it intends to meet and has five years to acquire stock or assets that do not exceed any upper limit on the threshold. 16 CFR § 801.1(h).

A filing starts a mandatory 30-day waiting period. If the either the DOJ or the FTC issues a request for additional information (the second request), the request tolls the waiting period. Once the parties have complied with the request, for most transactions, the federal agencies have 30 days to review the materials. The penalty can be up to $11,000 per day for failure to make a timely filing.

CHAPTER 14

ACQUISITIONS OF UNITED STATES CORPORATIONS BY FOREIGN COMPANIES

§ 48. The Exon-Florio Amendment of 1988

Congress passed the Exon-Florio Amendment to stop acquisitions of United States companies in defense-related industries. The Act authorizes the President of the United States to block acquisitions in the name of "national security." Treasury Regulations have created an interagency committee (CFIUS) to aid the President in exercising his discretion. 32 C.F.R. §§ 800 et seq. (1998).

The key term "national security" is undefined. The only guidance offered regarding the interpretation of national security appears in the commentary to the proposed regulations. The commentary adopts the interpretation found in the Congressional Conference Report to the Omnibus Trade and Competitiveness Act, which states simply that the "term 'national security' is intended to be interpreted broadly without limitation to particular industries," allowing the President or his designee to review transactions on a case-by-case basis. The commentary, also incorporated in the amendment's preamble, states that the "intent of the regulations is to indicate that notice, while voluntary, [is] clearly appropriate when, for example, a company is being acquired that provides products or key technologies essential to the U.S. defense industrial base." The lack of definition irks foreign governments who view the Act as a potential government licensing system for foreign direct investment in the United States. Japan, in trade negotiations, continually requests that the United States make the term specific.

In practice, CFIUS has recommended that the President block only one takeover and threatened to block one or two others (the threats stopped the deals).

The Act has international trade ramifications—making it more difficult for United States companies that want to make foreign direct investments abroad—and domestic industrial implications, prohibiting, for example, the Japanese from running a United States plant more efficiently than its United States owners.

§ 49. Federal Legislation Specific to Foreign Acquisitions in Particular Industries or of Particular Assets

The United States Congress has passed a series of laws that regulate foreign ownership (and therefore foreign acquisitions of domestic businesses) in specific industries. Some states, notably California, Iowa, New Mexico and Pennsylvania, may also restrict foreign ownership of certain types of property and the exploitation of natural resources by foreign investors.

The following list of federal acts focuses only on those that restrict not only the activity of foreign entities but also the activity of domestic entities (those incorporated in the United States) owned by foreign citizens or entities. The list is not exhaustive.

The *Foreign Bank Supervision Enhancement Act* of 1991 establishes special clearance and oversight criteria for foreign-owned banks that do business in the United States. 12 U.S.C. § 3105(d). The *Federal Communications Act* of 1934 bars foreign persons, entities or governments and United States entities controlled by foreign interests from possessing a broadcast or common carrier license unless the FCC determines it will serve the "public interest." 47 U.S.C. § 310(b). The *Communications Satellite Act* of 1962 restricts foreign ownership of wireless satellite communications networks. 47 U.S.C. §§ 201-04. The *Merchant Marine Act* of 1920 provides that merchandise moving between United States ports must be transported on United States built, owned and registered vessels. 46 U.S.C. app. § 883. The *Coast Guard Authorization Act* of 1989 limits direct or indirect foreign investment in our commercial fishing industry. 46 U.S.C. § 12102(c). The *Mineral Lands Leasing Act* of 1920 allows the

Secretary of the Interior to grant federal leases to develop natural resources in the United States to companies with larger than 10 percent foreign ownership only if United States citizens can obtain similar licenses or leases from the home governments of the foreign interests. 30 U.S.C. § 181. The *Atomic Energy Act* of 1954 effectively bars foreign ownership of companies that operate in the nuclear power industry, 42 U.S.C. § 2133(d), and foreign ownership of companies that mine uranium on public lands. 42 U.S.C. § 2097.

Numerous federal laws also establish specific disclosure requirements for foreign investors. Again, the following list is not exhaustive. The *International Investment and Trade in Services Survey Act* of 1976 requires United States corporations to report to the Department of Commerce within 45 days of the acquisition by a foreign person or entity of a 10 percent or larger voting equity interest if the stock acquired is valued at more than $1 million or if the corporation has annual sales, assets or net income of greater than $10 million. 22 U.S.C. § 3101-3108; see also 15 C.F.R. 806 (Commerce Department regulations). The Act also requires reports when an existing United States company that has a foreign investor who holds 10 percent or more of its voting stock acquires additional United States businesses. The *Foreign Investment and Real Property Tax Act* of 1989 gives the Secretary of the Treasury the power to require reporting by foreign persons or entities holding direct investments in

United States real estate having an aggregate fair market value in excess of $450,000. 26 U.S.C. § 6039C. The *Agricultural Foreign Investment Disclosure Act* of 1978 requires foreign persons or entities or domestic entities in which a foreigner holds 10 percent or more of the equity to file a report within 90 days before purchasing an interest in United States farming, ranching or timberland. 7 U.S.C. §§ 3501-3508.

INDEX

References are to Pages